Enjoy

Bernie Kanner

Are You Normal

About

Money?

Are You Normal

About

Money?

Do You Behave Like Everyone Else?

by Bernice Kanner

Bloomberg Press
Princeton

This publication contains the author's opinions and is designed to provide accurate and authoritative information. It is sold with the understanding that the author, publisher, and Bloomberg L.P. are not engaged in rendering legal, accounting, investment-planning, or other professional advice. The reader should seek the services of a qualified professional for such advice; the author, publisher, and Bloomberg L.P. cannot be held responsible for any loss incurred as a result of specific investments or planning decisions made by the reader.

First edition published 2001

1 3 5 7 9 10 8 6 4 2

Library of Congress Cataloging-in-Publication Data

Kanner, Bernice.
    Are you normal about money? : do you behave like everyone else? / Bernice Kanner.
        p. cm.
    ISBN 1-57660-087-4 (alk. paper)
    1. Money--United States--Psychological aspects. 2. Finance, Personal--United States. I. Title.

HG222.3 .K36 2001
332.024--dc21   2001037365

Edited by Rhona Ferling
Book design by Barbara Diez Goldenberg

Contents

Acknowledgments

Deep gratitude to the Bloomberg team—including, but not limited to, Bill Inman, Jared Kieling, Rhona Ferling, Tracy Tait, Priscilla Treadwell, and Dan Coffey—for making the merger of money and normalcy fun.

Are You Normal

About

Money?

Introduction

When did it happen that we left sex behind to dream of money—when money became the new sex? Indeed, watching people make money has been likened to the new voyeurism—what with *Greed* and Regis Philbin's *Who Wants to Be a Millionaire* assuming the status of national obsessions. In the twenty-first century, it's not religion that's the opiate of the people but making moolah. More Americans than ever are in the stock market, and newspaper readers often scan the business pages before they even check out the headline news.

But money, while it may be our national passion, hardly means the same thing to all of us. It never has. Way back in 42 B.C., Publilius Syrus declared its importance: "Money alone sets all the world in motion."

Ecclesiastes 10:19 declared that the buck stops here: "A feast is made for laughter, and wine maketh merry; but money answereth all things." And William Somerset Maugham in *Of Human Bondage* likened it to "a sixth sense without which you cannot make a complete use of the other five."

Others through history have pooh-poohed its meaning. "Money is not the be-all and end-all," Iszak Walton chided in *The Compleat Angler*. There are far more important things, such as health and good conscience. Those are blessings, Walton warned, "that money cannot buy."

But there are many blessings that money can buy. If we could have any luxury in the world, more of us would lavish money on a butler or maid than on anything else. Eighty-six percent of us who own pets buy them holiday gifts. We spend more feeding our cars than feeding ourselves. Thirteen percent of us almost always give to beggars.

Money can also cause a lot of rifts and tears. It's the leading cause of disagreements in marriages—and 44 percent of couples say differences in spending styles could prompt them to call the whole thing off. Two out of three swear they wouldn't sign a prenup. One-fifth of us have let a friendship dribble away over money. And for all the talk about equality, two out of five think that when it comes to a date, it's the guy who should pay.

I've spent the past year asking Americans on the Bloomberg Web site if they'd secretly rather visit a teller than an ATM (dream on); whether they use the soap bar down to the scuzz (many amalgamate it into the new bar to be sure they get their money's worth); and what they do with their loose change (forget the Great Wall of China: most of us have the Great Wad of Currency).

I've learned a lot about how we stretch it (44 percent reuse the tinfoil); procure it (40 percent have stayed in a job they hate because of the money); invest it (38 percent won't put their money in socially irresponsible companies); save it (only 52 percent have savings outside of a work-related plan); store it (the piggy bank is second to a glass jar); and worry about it (56 percent haven't been able to sleep because of it).

I also know what we'd do for it: Sixty-five percent would live on a deserted island for a year for a cool $1 million. Sixty percent would even take the rap for someone else and serve six months in jail for that amount—and 10 percent would lend their spouse for a night. For $10 million, most of us would do just about anything:

one-fourth would abandon our friends, our family, and our church. An equal number would change their race or sex. And for that kind of loot, 7 percent—one in every fourteen of us—would even murder.

I've turned to other sources to find the basics—when we lost our fiscal virginity (by sixteen, most of us have a savings account, and by twenty, a checking account); whether we pay our credit-card balance in full (49 percent of us do so each month); whether we own stock options (12 million of us do); and whether we pay our taxes voluntarily (the IRS claims 83 percent of us do).

But I'm more interested in what we're saying under our breaths—how we really feel and act and what money really means to us. Dip in and find out how you compare to everyone else. When it comes to money, are you normal?

chapter 1

Loose Change

M arketers have long divided consumers into "psychographic" groups according to their zip code, income, and such threads as their interest in ball games or ballet and their propensity to wear mascara or vote as a Democrat or Republican. They've served up different products and promotions to respond to our shopping and spending styles: all natural, economy size, two-for-one specials, top-of-the-line.

But no one has really classified us according to how we feel about money. Perhaps the next generation clue masters will be more subtle: Mr. Lavish Tipper; Ms. Spendthrift; Miss Tightwad ...

What's more fun: making money or spending it?
Big surprise: more people get a kick out of making money than from spending it (40 percent to 22 percent). Just 39 percent of us are in the total serenity zone—experiencing equal joy from the taking in and giving out of money.

Can you spend on others as easily as you do on yourself?
Thirteen percent say no way, José—they can treat themselves more easily than splurge on others.

Can money buy happiness?
Just 13 percent of us believe that it can, with men slightly more likely to subscribe to this than women. Yet one out of four people would
prefer wealth to having their family together and healthy. Ninety-
two percent would rather be rich than find the love of their lives.

What best describes your attitude toward money?
For 60 percent of us, it's security and independence. Thirty-seven
percent consider it a tool to accomplish some of life's goals. Two
percent equate it with power, while almost 1 percent associate having it with happiness.

If your money could talk to you, what would it say?
"We have fun together, but you don't respect me." That's the message that 46 percent of us think our dollars would send us, irked
that we treat them so cavalierly. Sixteen percent expect bills would
whine about being squeezed too tightly to breathe. And 38 percent
think their money would boast about being the one in charge.

Which do you think about more: sex or money?
Almost half of us (47 percent) think more about the almighty
dollar than their almighty lover, while 17 percent say they think
more about sex. For the rest it's pretty much a draw. Men (big
surprise here) are likelier than women to think more about sex—
or claim to.

OK, so which do you *enjoy* more?
Just 35 percent say that hands down, they enjoy sex more than they
enjoy money.

**Forget about sex, which do you talk about more: drugs
or money?**
Twenty-nine percent say their families have discussed their illegal
drug use, compared to 27 percent who admit they've talked about
their investments.

Have you ever been a member of a class-action suit?

Three out of five of us (58.6 percent) have never participated in a class-action suit but don't feel averse to doing so. Just 15.5 percent consider these suits rapacious and say it would be a cold day in July before they'd join one. More than one out of ten (11 percent) have benefited or expect to reap monetary rewards from a class-action suit, while 15 percent have participated but have found that it hasn't amounted to a hill of beans.

Would you give the bride and groom matri-money?

You can be fairly sure they want it, although it probably won't show up on the Williams-Sonoma gift registry: ninety-four percent of engaged couples would be tickled to open a gift that says "Pay to the Order of ..." At least it won't be one of the 10 percent of traditional wedding gifts that go back to the store, often to pay wedding expenses. Most newlyweds start their marriages in debt.

One-third of people—35 percent—say they wouldn't spend the time and energy to get a refund for anything less than a dollar. Twenty percent say they'd take the trouble for anything over $2 or $3. Eighteen percent consider $5 to be motivation enough, whereas 14 percent wouldn't put themselves out for anything shy of $10. Fewer than 1 percent say any overcharge puts them in motion, whereas 3 percent say no amount of money would induce them to try to get their money back.

What would you do with money given to you as a gift that had been illicitly gained through stealing or inflicting pain and suffering?

Four out of ten people—44 percent—would keep it, while an

almost equal number—42 percent—say they'd give the money to charity or in some other way put it to use to alleviate a world problem. Sixteen percent have other plans for the dough—some perhaps better left unsaid.

Ever made a money decision based on a horoscope or a fortune-teller?

When it comes to money, 91 percent of us claim to be totally rational. Just 9 percent admit they've relied on celestial guidance.

Figure your income will greatly influence how your kids turn out?

Two-fifths—41 percent—suspect that their income and attendant lifestyle will greatly influence what their children turn out to be like. Some 56 percent downplay it, and 3 percent are fence-sitters.

Is money the biggest factor in chalking up professional success?

Only 19 percent of us admit that money is the big kahuna. The rest attribute success to other factors such as character and ambition.

Do you value money more than you'd like to admit?

Just shy of two-thirds of us—65 percent—figure we've got the right outlook about money. But one-third admit to putting too much weight on it.

How big a stress is moolah in your life?

It's the biggest: right up there with job and career pressure for 22 percent of us. Close on those heels as stress generators are time pressures (19 percent) and (gasp!) family life (18 percent). Their love life or the absence of it is stressing out 8 percent of Americans.

Did you grow up believing that money was dirty?

Your mother should know. When Saint Paul argued in his first epistle to Timothy that "filthy lucre" was the root of all evil, Mom knew he wasn't kidding. She told you never to trust its sanitary conditions or put it near your mouth. (After all, you don't know where it's been.) A study in *Infections in Medicine* found that 3 percent of coins and 11 percent of bills are growing bacteria. In Japan, ATM maker Hitachi lets you get your money "laundered"—that is, briefly pressed between rollers at high enough temperatures to kill many bacteria. Too bad so few of us have a Howard Hughes complex.

Do you believe in Horatio Alger?
Over half of us—59 percent—believe that by sufficiently applying elbow grease, you can succeed. Twelve percent believe the road to riches is paved with family wealth, and no amount of effort will change that.

Where'd you learn what you know about money?
Seven out of ten people claim to be self-taught about money. Most (54 percent) say they learned how to manage it from friends and relatives. Less than half turn to financial professionals.

At the time Darva Conger said "I do," did you think it would last?
Initially, one out of four TV viewers—24 percent—gave the bride who wanted to marry a multimillionaire and her groom, Rick Rockwell, less than one year.

Have you ever traded stuff?
Three out of four of us have swapped items offline, but only 4.6 percent have traded on eBay.

Do you believe the meek shall inherit the earth?
People may be getting and spending like there's no tomorrow, but 52 percent of us still believe that the meek shall inherit the earth. According to Alden & Associates, a Hermosa Beach, California-based marketing research firm, women (60 percent) were likelier than men (39 percent) to feel that way. The same is true for Southerners (62 percent) compared to Northeasterners (37 percent). Two-thirds (65 percent) of those with household incomes

under $30,000 are pinning their hopes on meekness coming out on top, while just 39 percent of those whose household incomes are over $75,000 are relying on that.

Can you tell if the price is right?
Slightly less than half of us can correctly guess the price of items we often buy within fifteen seconds of putting them in our grocery carts.

Do you have a budget?
Some 43 percent of us claim we stick to a monthly budget most or all of the time. An equal number haven't even established one.

Is there such a thing as a free lunch?
Slightly more than one in every ten of us believes there really is such a thing as a free lunch. Almost half—44.9 percent—take a more cautious view, believing that ultimately the price smacks you in the face.

When it comes to money matters, how do you assess your skill?
More than half of all investors believe they have a better than average chance of beating the market—though that's not likely.

Do you often throw good money after bad?
More often than we want to admit. Forty percent of people admit that they avoid finalizing and accepting losses, so they'll spend hundreds of dollars to fix an old car just because they've already spent a lot on it. Or they'll hold on to a stinky stock not because they think it will soar again but because they don't want to admit to themselves that they picked a dud.

Truthfully, how would you feel if your neighbor or coworker struck it rich?
There is no black and white in this world, only gray. Three out of five of us—59 percent—expect they'd feel a combination of envy

and joy. Eighteen percent said it would be pure joy (wonder if they're related to their neighbor), but 15 percent admit they'd predominantly feel envy.

What do you do when someone asks how much you've paid for something?

Though we've been taught it's rude to ask, three out of five of us—59.7 percent—tell the truth. Just one in ten of us—though three times as many Northeasterners as Westerners—say "It's none of your business." An equal number would feign ignorance. One in ten of us would outright lie.

Deep down, do you like rich people better than poor ones?

Almost half (47.7 percent) of those queried insist that their feelings for someone are not based on money, but almost one-third—29 percent—are totally candid people and say that they probably do like wealthier folks better. A fourth plead the Fifth, clamming up on this ever so politically incorrect assessment.

How fast does money flow through your hands?

Forty-four percent of folks say they shell it out almost as quickly as they make it, while 14 percent try to squirrel away as much money as they can. Forty-one percent try to balance the scale.

Ever asked for an item free if it rings wrong at the cash register?

Almost one-third (31 percent) of folks claim they didn't know you could. Meanwhile, roughly equal amounts of people—between 22 and 23 percent—have decided it's not worth it as have decided that it is. Sixteen percent say they'd be too embarrassed, while 7 percent, apprised of this opportunity, now plan to seize it.

Do you expect to help your kids financially?

Sixty-four percent of moms and 71 percent of dads believe they'll be chipping in for their child's first car. One-fourth of women and 38 percent of men expect to help pay for Junior's first home.

Do you expect to help your parents financially?
More than nine out of ten respondents still have at least one living parent or parent-in-law. But only 13 percent expect to provide some financial support to them.

How much would it take to make a real difference in your life?
One-third of us say that an extra $100,000 in the bank would noticeably improve our lot. For 14 percent, it would take at least $500,000. An even $1 million would shake things up for 16 percent of us, and 24 percent calculate it would take at least $10 million to change their lives significantly.

What is poor?
Most of us consider a family of four with household income of $35,000 or less to be poor, but that's twice the U.S. government's threshold for poverty (about $17,000 a year). In a recent year, the median household income in the United States wasn't far from that: $38,900.

Ever been the victim of a financial scam?
Just 4 percent of us have been—or will acknowledge it.

Have you set up a trust or are you the recipient of one?
We should all be so lucky, but just 28.4 percent of us are. Two-thirds (67.6 percent) may have trust envy but no fund, while 4 percent have no idea whether that's in their cards.

If you had a trust fund, would you tell people?
One-third (32.8 percent) of us wouldn't, and 42.8 percent would only tell intimates.

Need financial help? Who you gonna call?

Most people expect that if they're ever down-and-out they'd get tide-me-over money from family members (88.4 percent) or friends (69.8 percent). But just 43.3 percent of needy folks have actually gotten help from their families and 17.2 percent from friends.

Do you buy extended warranties on major appliances?

The salesman who tries to sell these is in for a lot of rejection. Four-fifths of us avoid it because we've read that it's not a wise investment. Eight percent occasionally fall under the spell of a persuasive salesman.

What's the lowest price for a bra you'd find excessive?

Apparently we're not used to spending big on bras. More than one-third of us (38.3 percent) say $30 is too much, while another 28.4 percent say $50 is way overboard. Ten percent would go as high as $75, and 3.5 percent would shell out $100. But 19.8 percent say the sky's the limit, considering what they're encasing.

Have you ever walked away from money?

One out of every eight of us mistakenly has left assets at some point, according to the National Association of Unclaimed Property Administrators. The average amount is $1,000, but collectively it adds up to more than $14 billion. The biggest repositories: bank accounts, payroll checks that were never cashed, uncollected IRS refunds, forgotten stock, and unredeemed utility and rental deposits.

Do you show love and appreciation by buying big gifts?

Three out of five (59 percent) of us deny that we do. But 35 percent own up to it. Six percent claim not to know what qualifies as "big."

Ever go to investment seminars?

More than two out of five of us (42 percent) say they eagerly attend them to hear different viewpoints.

Which feeling is the strongest, hatred for losing money or enjoyment of winning it?
Optimism reigns. More than half of us say the pleasure experienced from getting money far outweighs the pain of losing it.

Is your money ready when the cashier announces the amount?
Most of us have been taught that good manners mean not keeping the rest of the queue waiting. So it's not surprising that more than two out of every three of us (68.9 percent) have our money in hand when the total is announced.

How much time do you spend handling money?
No wonder we don't get enough sleep. On average, we spend 7 percent of our lives handling money matters. Still, 4 percent say they'd like to spend even more.

Ever been burned by a financial "adviser"?
Get the healing ointment. Just like the surgeon who's supposed to help but leaves the scalpel inside his patient, a so-called financial adviser has taken 23 percent of us to the cleaners.

Have you set up a power of attorney?
Only 28 percent of us have.

Growing up, how was money regarded in your family?
It's the ghost in the attic. In a third of families (31 percent), nobody spoke about money, while in 45 percent they constantly worried about the way they spent it.

If you won the lottery how would you take the money?
More than three out of four (76.1 percent) would take the lump sum and run. Nineteen percent would opt for an annual payment.

What's the first thing you ever bought with your own money?
Most of us don't remember (48.6 percent). But of those who do, 18.6 percent recall that it was candy, while 8.7 percent each conjure up images of their first purchase as being a book, a comic book, or a toy.

Would you have as a goal to spend your last dollar the day you die?
To 15 percent of us, that notion sounds real good. But 61.3 percent say it sounds hedonistic and selfish. One-fourth—23.8 percent—don't know how to react to it, not wanting to think about a day when they and their bank accounts will be parted.

Ever accepted an airline's offer to give up your seat for money?
Eighteen percent have declined the chance because their time is more valuable—but 44 percent have never had the opportunity.

When you played Monopoly®, what was your favorite property?
Parker Brothers, are you listening? The dominant strategy is not to buy the utilities first (just 13 percent of us do that) or go for the greens first (a tactic favored by only 3.9 percent) or the yellows (1.9 percent) or even restrict ourselves to a few properties and put hotels everywhere (24.5 percent). Rather, it's to "buy whatever I land on," an approach preferred by 56.6 percent of players.

If you were offered a free trip to a weekend resort as long as you attended a 90-minute sales pitch for a time-share, would you go?
Some of us must be agreeing to go, or all those high-pressure pitches wouldn't keep coming. Yet 63.2 percent of folks say they'd tell the caller they're not interested and mean it. Twenty-two percent would go along for the ride and act interested, while 8 percent claim they'd come clean and tell the caller upfront that they don't want the time-share but would happily accept the trip. Another

8 percent say they'd go on the trip and try to get out of attending the sales pitch.

If it were coming out of your own pocket, would you prefer a generic drug or its costlier name-brand version?
Most of us (51 percent) would go for the generic, but 21 percent would rather be safe than sorry and go for the name brand.

When a broker cold-calls to solicit your account, what do you do?
No wonder the phone is always ringing. One-third of recipients invite the cold-callers to send them information. Four percent do something more aggressively mean than hanging up.

Is it wrong for a rich politician to spend his own money lavishly on an election?
Almost two-thirds of us (63.9 percent) say all's fair in a democracy, and better that politicians spend their money than ours. Some 13.6 percent feel it's buying an election and it's wrong.

Do you haunt tag sales?
Forty percent of us do. Seven percent usually pay the posted price, but 14.2 percent always haggle for a better deal.

When you're someone's guest at a restaurant, are you timid or tenacious?
Some 68.7 percent select something in the middle. Just 12.6 percent say they'd opt for one of the least expensive entrees, and less than 1 percent would pick one of the most expensive entrees. Nearly one-fifth (18 percent) would order whatever they wanted, oblivious of the cost.

When the restaurant bill comes, how do you most often react?
Half of us (50.7 percent) study the bill but will point out only a

major discrepancy, while 43 percent give their credit card or money with a mere perfunctory glance. Just 6.4 percent admit they scrutinize the tab and point out any errors.

What would you do if you found $20 in a pair of pants you haven't worn recently?
Where's the fun? Three-fourths of us (75.8 percent) treat it as they would any other money: they forget about it. Just 10 percent would blow it on something frivolous, and 14.6 percent would save it.

Would you rather personally strike it rich but have a nation at war, or enjoy peace without any personal prosperity?
What we'd personally like to do is compromise. Two-thirds of us (68 percent) wonder if some middle ground isn't possible. Failing that, 12 percent would rather be rich and at war, but 20 percent magnanimously say they'd rather be poor and have their nation at peace.

Would you rather buy a last-minute fare for half price and risk not going or pay full fare for a guaranteed seat?
Only 7.9 percent of us would take the gamble on the risky bargain. Almost 14 percent would secure a seat at any price; 58.6 percent would decide based on how important the event was; and 19.7 percent would let the price differential sway them.

Given the opportunity, do you usually buy duty-free stuff?
More than half of us steer clear of duty-free goods. Some 28.9 percent avoid the duty-free shop because they don't consider it any bargain, and 23.3 percent don't want to carry the loot. Some 27.7 percent occasionally stock up, and 20.1 percent seize the moment whenever they can.

Was Robin Hood a hero or a fiend?
Roughly the same number of people consider the guy who stole from the rich and gave to the poor a hero (27.4 percent) as regard him a thief (25.5 percent). Almost one in ten sees him as a "misguided soul who needs social reconditioning."

What would you do with food in your fridge past the date stamped on it?
Ugh! Almost half of us (45.2 percent) would throw it out immediately. An almost equal number (39.3 percent) say if it wasn't rotten, they'd eat it anyway. Two percent would even scrape off mold and go at it, while 13.7 percent protest that it depends on how badly needed the item was (and how inconvenient it would be to replace).

If a dinner partner tried to explain the pros and cons of term life insurance to you, what would you most likely do?
Civility reigns. Only 2.8 percent of us would take the hostess aside and then go for her jugular. More than half—56.4 percent—would try to tactfully change the subject to something nonfinancial, and 16 percent would engage in the discussion or expand it to, say, REITs or derivatives. Another 22.4 percent would try to listen attentively, while 3 percent of desperadoes would hole up in the bathroom.

chapter 2

Chintzing

E ven in boom times, many of us were trimming expenses. In the face of a heady stock market, three out of four people admitted that they had cut back in the past year, nearly one-third of them by more than 10 percent. You may not go so far as to reuse the lint from the clothes dryer, but there are other ways to stretch a dollar. Just how far are you prepared to go?

Do you consider yourself cheap?

Some 11 percent of men and 8 percent of women consider themselves, well, frugal. Many more call themselves "value-conscious." Just 2 percent of folks accept the designation "tightwad." (Four times as many define themselves as spendthrifts.)

Okay, just how frugal are you?

Let's put it this way: one in ten of us admit we pour the contents from the cheaper store-label or generic bottle into the costlier brand-name containers. Some 57 percent of us reuse wrapping paper, and 44 percent reuse tinfoil.

Is "Never pay retail" your eleventh commandment?

Half of us—54 percent—admit that buy-on-sale is our mantra, that we always look for a bargain. Thirty-nine percent consider those who pay full price to be dolts. Fewer than 10 percent describe themselves as so time-poor that price is irrelevant.

Forty-two percent of us admit we chintz on things that other people can't see, like wearing torn underwear.

What's your worst financial gaffe?

For 41 percent of us, we feel like we've been had if we've overpaid for something.

Do you usually buy the cheapest seats at a ball game or theater and then try to scoot up to better ones?

Where's the adventurous spirit? More than three-fourths of us (76.5 percent) say we'd rather shell out more to be sure we'll have good seats than take our chances and pocket the savings. Only 9.3 percent of us try this self-designed upgrade exclusively at ball games, while 2 percent do it only at the theater. Twelve percent do it anywhere and enjoy their seats more for the fun of securing them.

Would you take the lightbulbs when you move?

Maybe *you* wouldn't, but lots of folks out there are making off with them. Four out of ten home buyers find that previous owners have removed lightbulbs, ostensibly in an effort to save money. And 23 percent of new home owners have discovered that light fittings and fixtures have also been carried off by the previous tenants.

How often do you switch car insurers to save on the premiums?

Seventy-one percent of us say we switch at least once a year to trim costs. But for most of us there's got to be at least a 20 percent savings on what we're currently paying before we'll switch.

During the past year, have you avoided seeing a doctor, counselor, dentist, or other health-care provider because of the cost?
Some 27 percent have forgone medical care because of the expense. Folks without insurance and those with annual incomes below $30,000 are likelier to suffer in silence. But 21 percent of those with health insurance have done the same. And surprisingly, nearly one in five people with incomes over $60,000 are likely to pull the stiff upper lip, put off by the complicated system of deductibles, copayments, and coinsurance.

Do you regularly call hotels or magazines to negotiate better rates?
Four out of ten say when they're footing the bill, they regularly get on the horn with hotels and/or magazines to negotiate better rates.

Have you switched credit cards to pay lower fees?
One in four of us has switched credit cards in the last year to pay a lower interest rate or avoid a high annual fee.

Do you often plan meals around a grocery store's specials?
Only one in five of us decides that if ground beef is on sale, hamburgers are on the menu (barring Mad Cow Disease, of course).

Do you usually get rain checks on out-of-stock sale merchandise?
For 40.5 percent of us, waiting to be issued rain checks for sold-out stuff is just too much effort. The rest sometimes or always do.

Do you add water to the nearly empty bottle of tomato sauce to coax as much out as possible?
At least two-thirds of us say diluting with water ruins the taste. But 14 percent regularly nudge the dregs out that way and consider doing otherwise to be pure wasteful foolishness.

Do you turn off lights when you leave a room?

Just 1.5 percent of us believe that when God said "Let there be light," he meant all the time. On the other hand, 31 percent claim they conscientiously turn off lights, but more to save energy than dollars. Thirty-four percent flip them off because ohms add up.

Would you drive farther for cheaper gasoline?

Some 15.7 percent of us would pull in at the nearest gas station whenever the fuel tank was low. But one-third (33.6 percent) go a little out of their way for cheaper gas, and 44 percent would decide whether it was worth the time and effort based on the difference in price. Some 6.6 percent absolutely would take the trouble on principle.

Do you take home the leftovers from a restaurant meal?

About 62 percent of Americans do. More women than men (67 percent versus 56 percent) ask for doggie bags, but guys are likelier than gals to scarf it down later (91 percent versus 86 percent). Higher-income folks tend to ask their waiters to wrap it up, perhaps because they go to restaurants that serve better food—and who wants to waste a pricey meal?

Do you usually go for the bargain or the best?

Sixty-two percent say they'd go for the very best. Men were markedly less interested in the good bargain (22 percent) than women were (42 percent) and correspondingly more likely to say they want the very best (men, 70 percent; women, 53 percent).

Do you reuse tea bags?

More than two-thirds of us (68 percent) say that's going too far. But 23.6 percent insist that one tea bag contains more than enough tea to flavor a whole pot.

Do you roll the toothpaste tube to squeeze the most out of it?
"Doesn't everybody?" wonder 59.5 percent of us.

Do you make extra ice cubes before a party rather than buying them?
Twenty-seven percent say that's way too much work, while 7 percent say they'd like to but are usually too disorganized to get around to it.

When your purchase yields a penny in change, what do you do?
We may leave a penny on the street and not bother to bend for it, but when the cashier puts it—and nothing else—in our hand, more than half of us take it.

When it comes to soap, what's your personality?
Twenty-four percent try to meld the remnants of the old bar into a new one.

Do you fill the gas tank before returning a rental car in order to pay less?
Thirteen percent don't bother, despite the fact that they pay a hefty convenience fee for not filling up.

Would you stay over Saturday night to pay less airfare?
Fifty-nine percent of us would definitely spend the night away from home to save on airfare if it were doable.

chapter 3

Cash Cache

M ost of us make, on average, three transactions a day involv-
ing coins. We touch on average $600 in change a year, and
15 percent count the money in their wallets at least once a
day. How do you handle the actual stuff?

How much do you usually carry around?
The average wallet contains $104 and change.

Where do you carry it?
Just 61 percent of men carry a wallet—fewer in the city than in
the country—though 96 percent of women do. One out of five
men throws his money loose in his pockets. Six percent carry a
money clip.

Is your wallet organized?
Reeeeeeaady, march! Almost three-fourths of us (72 percent) store
our bills in rigid order, with singles leading up to higher denomi-
nations. Northerners and baby boomers are considerably more
likely than Southerners to stow their paper money randomly.

Do you save old pennies?
We may not stoop on the street to pick them up, but more than half of us—52 percent—stash them away. Banks used to supply penny-roll "collars" free; now many charge for taking them off our hands.

How about other change?
Each of us has, on average, between $30 and $50 worth of change in our coat pockets, piggy banks, and glass jars. That amounts to more than $7 billion in change sitting idle across the nation.

Do you stockpile your change or religiously try to get rid of it?

Almost half of us—46.1 percent—would walk on by if we saw a penny lying on the asphalt. Fourteen percent would stoop for a nickel, but another 7.4 percent wouldn't bother for anything less than a dime. And for 15.2 percent, it costs 25¢ to bend those knees. Astonishingly, 8.4 percent of people wouldn't pick up anything short of a dollar.

Three-fourths of us tend to store up our spare change rather than try to get rid of it during our daily transactions, according to the Coinstar National Currency Poll. One-fourth of folks—23 percent—say they never do get around to using it.

Where do you stow your spare change?
Although piggy banks are the obvious place, only 13 percent of adults use them. More than twice as many (28 percent) opt for a glass or plastic jar. Others have converted assorted bottles and jugs, coffee cans, cookie tins, bowls, buckets, baskets, dresser or kitchen drawers, plastic bags, boxes, ashtrays, cigar boxes, fish tanks, or car compartments into coin receptacles.

How much change has to accumulate before you convert to bills?
Fourteen percent of us cash in our spare-change caches when the contents total $10 or less. Thirteen percent wait until it tops $30. Agewise, baby boomers are the biggest change stockpilers.

Do you squirrel dollar bills around the house?
More than half of us—53.1 percent—wonder why anyone would ever do that. But 7.3 percent say they do salt it away, and in some ingenious places at that, and 8 percent say they keep extra dough around but in obvious places. One-third of Americans—31.6 percent—say they keep only a small amount on hand for emergencies.

Should the U.S. mint stop making the penny?
More than half of us (53 percent) think pennies are a nuisance and want to give Lincoln a rest.

Have you ever received a counterfeit note?
Almost $32 million in counterfeit currency (out of a total $405 billion in circulation) was distributed nationwide in a recent year. Surprisingly, the bogus bills are more often $20s than $100s.

Do you abuse your money?
The government believes you do. Its paper bills (actually a rugged mix of 75 percent cotton and 25 percent linen) are made to take it—girded for 4,000 folds in each direction. However, the average U.S. dollar lasts a mere eighteen months, according to the Federal Reserve.

Should "In God We Trust" be on our coins?
Two-thirds of us (62.6 percent) say it should, but 18 percent claim to be affronted by this fusion of church and state.

Should the "E Pluribus Unum" on the coins be changed to English?
Three-fourths of us (75.8 percent) vote for the status quo.

Do you care if your bills are crisp?
You bet. A few of us (1.5 percent) have even ironed our money!

What do you do with a bill you've accidentally torn?
Tear, shmare. Almost all of us—89.6 percent—tape it and pass it on. Some 2.5 percent—diabolical folks—leave it in two parts as a tip!

Do you have a favorite when you call "heads" or "tails"?
People are three times likelier to call heads than they are to call tails.

Twenty-six percent of us jiggle the change in our pockets.

What do you do with foreign coins that look like ours but are worth less—like Canadian coins?
Two-thirds of us (63.1 percent) save the currency as a souvenir. One-fourth (25.8 percent) try to pass it off as American currency, and 39 percent say they'd leave it as a tip.

Ever refused to accept money or had it refused because it was dirty?
Stained, wrinkled, even mutilated, it seems that when it comes to money, looks play second fiddle. Seventy-eight percent of us have never spurned money that was filthy, although 20 percent say they try to get rid of the grungy stuff first. Nearly 10 percent say they've had dirty money refused.

Do you prefer to carry more small bills or fewer big bills?
More of us (44.2 percent) prefer to tote around a combination. Twenty-eight percent carry as little cash as possible.

If you were withdrawing $200 from an ATM, what denominations would you prefer?
We may carry around lots of fives and tens, but we secretly prefer twenty-dollar bills.

Do you ever count your money in front of people?
We all grew up on admonishments not to count our money in public, but only 39 percent of us profess to be extremely careful about this. Another 43 percent say they sometimes count their dough in the bank but do not flash it. The rest think nothing of it.

Have you ever had your pocket picked or your wallet stolen?
More than one in five people (21.2 percent) have been the victim of this costly, irritating crime.

Do you keep your money and credit cards separate?
If you get pickpocketed, you're in a whole heap of trouble if you don't, but just 46 percent of us keep them segregated.

Have you ever thrown out or torn up money in anger?
Money is sacred, say 95 percent of us. But more than 2 percent admit they've shed some dough in anger.

chapter 4

Whatcha Got?

Main Street has merged with Wall Street. More of us than ever before are in the market. Fifty-eight percent now own stocks or bonds, and 52 percent, mutual funds. Forty-three percent own savings bonds, 36 percent have CDs, 21 percent have a money market account, and 54 percent are covered by some sort of pension plan. Six percent have personal annuities or trusts. Just one in twenty-five have no investments at all.

Are all your eggs in one basket?

Not likely. Most of us have a few baskets, but our homes are clearly the Humpty Dumpties that we don't want to have fall. They represent 66 percent of total assets for the median U.S. household. Removing that from the equation, more people have their "eggs" sorted among savings (29 percent) than anywhere else, followed by IRAs, 401(k)s, and pension plans (20 percent). Nine percent have the bulk of their money in mutual funds, and 8 percent have it in stocks or bonds. Five percent have it in life insurance, and 4 percent in CDs. Twenty-six percent have it in some other cache or equally mixed among at least two forms.

Where it's stored is often a function of where the storer is on the financial totem pole.

What's the best way to get rich today?

That depends on how much you already have. Those earning at least $100,000 a year figure the road to riches is paved by starting a business (26 percent), followed by investing in stocks (22 percent) and real estate (15 percent). Those earning less bet on land, followed by starting their own business. The least wealthy hitch their wagon to inheriting money, compared to the middle class, who put their faith largely in the stock market.

When did you lose your investment virginity?

On average, men buy their first stock, bond, or mutual fund at around age twenty-seven, two to three years before the average woman does. The average age to purchase an annuity for the first time is forty-nine, and 90 percent of people still own the first annuity they ever bought.

Do you consider the moral, social, or environmental implications of your investments?

Two out of five investors (38 percent) avoid involvement with socially irresponsible companies. Almost as many (35 percent) only care about the return: "Show me the money" is their mantra.

Do you feel comfortable about your ability to earn back any money you lose?

Despite Nasdaq's gyrations, there's a real sense of confidence in the economy. More than half of us believe we can regain any losses without much pain. Only 7 percent have significant doubts that they'll rebound bigger and better than ever.

Feet to the fire, could you name one company in which your mutual funds are invested?

Two out of three mutual fund owners aren't even able to name one.

Would you rather pick a car or a fund?
We all consider a job interview more stressful than choosing a mutual fund, and the craps tables at Las Vegas more hazardous. But twice the number of people who don't own funds feel much more confident choosing a new car than choosing a fund.

Do you care if it's loaded?
Almost half of mutual fund owners (47 percent) will buy only funds that are no-load or have very low management fees or no redemption fees.

Do you really read the prospectus that comes with funds?
So what if the type's too small? Seventy-two percent of us don't even try.

In your household, who picks the stocks?
More than half of families (54 percent) share the workload. When one partner does it all, 28 percent of the time it's the guy in the director's chair, and 20 percent of the time, the gal.

How do you decide how to invest?
Twenty-nine percent of investors rely principally on financial newspapers and magazines for advice, while 18 percent consider what friends and relatives say to be their key source. Ten percent pay heed to financial advisers and experts, and 6 percent each to stockbrokers and their banker. Only 2 percent use company newsletters and reports to help with their decision making.

Have you ever bought stock on the basis of a so-called hot tip?
Forty-one percent of us consider "hot tips" useless hokum. But 22.4 percent consider them a cornerstone of their investment strategy. Three percent would like to trade on such pass-alongs but worry that it's illegal. One-third have never been fed any inside news.

Have you ever received a stock tip from a friend?
Friendship and money don't mix. Just one-third of us trade investment tips with our friends.

Have you ever engaged in pillow talk or other investment no-nos?
Two-thirds of us (65.3 percent) recognize that insider trading is serious business and are careful to keep kosher here. But 17 percent admit that they've "sort of" pushed the envelope. Six percent say they believe it's justified because everyone does it.

Ever invested in anything based on a message board or chat group?
Now that would be stupid, say 77.8 percent of us. But 8 percent consider it grassroots democracy in action. The rest are mum.

How long do you study the pool before jumping in?
Forty-two percent devote at least two hours to studying a stock before investing. Fifteen percent do little or no research at all.

Do you prefer to do it yourself or to have someone else to blame?
Two-thirds of us—66 percent—want to call the shots either individually or via someone in the family. The rest would rather leave the driving to a pro.

When you make money in the stock market, whom do you credit?
Some 45 percent of us credit a general rise in the economy—while 35 percent chalk it up to their own cleverness. Only 5 percent acknowledge their broker, and 15 percent tip their hats to luck.

When you lose money in the stock market, whom do you blame?
Half of us say the buck stops with ourselves, but 35 percent point

the finger at the overall economic decline and 12 percent at simple bad luck. Three percent blame an incompetent adviser.

How long do you usually hold a stock?

Recently, investors held Big Board stocks for just over eight months on average and Nasdaq stocks for five months. A decade ago, two years was the typical length of hold for both. On average, we hold mutual funds for four years versus ten years a decade ago.

What's a long-term investment to you?

Seventy percent of us define long-term as three years. For 23 percent it's one year; 7 percent say long-term can be three days, depending on the market's volatility.

How often do you check stock quotes?

Forty-one percent of us see if we're whole once a day; 18 percent—Nervous Nellies—do it, on average, three times a day; and 15 percent do so even more frequently. More laid-back souls (10 percent) check once a week or so, and 5 percent don't look more than once a month. Another 10 percent never check at all.

Do you generally panic and think about bailing in a downturn?

Borrowing a page from the Stoics, half of us admit we feel the

---

Risky Business...

Three-fourths of us (74.2 percent) have never sold stock short.

More than three out of four have never bought stocks on margin.

Fewer than 20 percent of us have ever bought commodities. Five percent don't even know what they are.

Seventy-five percent of investors routinely reinvest their stock dividends.

panic rising but force ourselves to stay the course. Another 33.5 percent claim we stay cool. Just 7 percent admit that the panic scenario nails us, and 9 percent say we avoid it altogether by not being in the market.

How aggressive a player are you?

Seventy percent of investors opt for safety: low risk and low return. Only 25 percent swing for the fences, while the rest mix it up.

Do you churn?

One in five—21 percent—let sleeping dogs lie, just slightly more than the 19 percent who change their investments annually or so. Eighteen percent meddle spontaneously, when circumstances dictate. For half of us, "circumstances" means a change in our personal financial condition; for one-fifth, it could be changes in interest rates.

Are you likelier to sell stocks that have gone up or down?

Most of us sell stocks that have gone up rather than tumbled.

> More than half of the people who trade online do so from their work desks.

Can you sell your losers as quickly as your winners?

Seems that it's emotionally easier to take a profit than a loss. Three-fifths of us (61.6 percent) find it easier to sell the winners, while for 11 percent, it's easier to sell the dogs.

Do you trade over the Internet?

The Web has certainly woven us in. Seventy-eight percent of investors use the Net to track their portfolios, 76 percent to research investments, and 70 percent to trade. Two out of three check their holdings daily on the Internet. The typical online investor makes twelve trades per month, averaging $40,000 each and costing $25 each in transaction fees.

Do you own stock options?

Somewhere between 7 million and 12 million U.S. workers do, with the National Center for Employee Ownership estimating on the low end and Oppenheimer Funds on the high. Either way, two out of five options owners admit they've no clue as to how they work.

Have you ever allowed your stock options to expire?

Around 11 percent of options owners have allowed profitable options to expire and become worthless.

Do you know whether you pay brokerage fees?

Sixty percent of us know we are, but only 30 percent know just what the fee is.

Do you try to shield capital gains?

Just 12 percent are feverishly doing so. Half of us (50.4 percent) have a tax shelter or two.

Have you ever set up a blind trust?

Fewer than 3 percent of us have ever done so.

What's the biggest fiscal blunder you've made in investing?

It may not be the biggest, but trying to time the market is the most common mistake investors make, followed by underutilizing corporate contributions and not contributing early enough.

Do you think you're beating the market?

Just as most people think of themselves as better-than-average-looking, most mutual fund holders see themselves as way ahead of the market. Researchers at Northwestern and Harvard found that 88 percent of investors overstated their actual returns.

chapter 5

Wanna Bet?

A recent survey found that one out of four Americans believe their best chance of getting rich is by playing the lottery—rather than by socking it away or investing in the stock market. Are you one of them?

Do you play?

Sixty-eight percent of us have gambled in the past year. Most walked away with less than we started with: collectively $50 billion less, and that's just counting legal wagering.

Which would you rather play: the IPO market or the craps table?

Seven out of ten people would rather take their chances on the IPO market. The rest consider the stock market the riskiest casino in the world and IPO synonymous with It's Probably Overpriced. What's more, there are no free cocktails at the roulette wheel of the stock market, and there's often a twenty-plus-pages backgrounder deigned must reading.

How about buying Internet stocks?

Nine percent of Americans bought Internet stocks recently, but few of them considered that "real" gambling.

Would you gamble half your net wealth for a 50 percent chance of quadrupling it?

Fewer than one in four (23 percent) say that sounds like solid mathematics to them. But 30 percent confess they'd put their entire net worth on the line for an 80 percent chance of multiplying it by ten.

Do you play the lottery?

Sixty-two percent of us have bought a lottery ticket at least once in our lives.

Five percent of players account for 51 percent of lottery-ticket sales.

Which is more compelling: better odds or a better jackpot?

Seventy-four percent of us claim we aren't influenced by the odds of winning nearly so much as we're drawn to play by the size of the jackpot. Good thing for the institutes that benefit, for the odds against pocketing a lottery jackpot are about 10 million to 1.

What do you play?

Instant games, such as scratch-offs, are the most popular type of "street chance," followed by the Wednesday and Saturday lotteries. Instant games score especially well with Gen Xers: Fifty-seven percent of them who play the lottery pick instant-win/lose games.

Where do you buy your lottery tickets?

Convenience stores and gas stations (60 percent). Supermarkets (22 percent) and liquor stores (8 percent).

Do you ever gamble at a casino?

Almost one-third of Americans—30 percent—say they've been to a casino some time in the past year.

What are you likely to play?

Blackjack is the game of choice. Some 42 percent of us prefer to play that above all other seductions. Another 32 percent are drawn to the slot machines, and 7.4 percent queue up for roulette.

If you were losing, would you pull out or hunker down?

Almost all of us (85 percent) head to the tables with a preset amount in our minds that we're willing to lose. But when we reach that limit, 11.7 percent gingerly go into reserves, and 3 percent profess to double their bet on the theory that luck turns.

> A person driving ten miles to buy a Lotto ticket is three times more likely to be killed in a car accident on the way there than to win the jackpot.

Are you a compulsive gambler?

Four percent of us—whether we own up to it or not—are.

Do you play sweepstakes?

Slightly fewer than 5 percent of us who receive a sweepstakes pitch in the mail actually respond to it. Players tend to come from all regions and income levels. The one thing they seem to have in common: a gambling twitch.

What's your take on the office betting pool?

You're probably not overly enthusiastic about the office or community betting pool. Only 7 percent join in any chance they get, while 51.4 percent hop on board if it comes our way. Interestingly, the more money we earn, the likelier we are to dive into this pool.

Bet you didn't know...

✳ ...One in five of us has played video poker in the past year.

✳ ...Only 13 percent bet on a professional sports event.

✳ ...Only 9 percent have ever bet on a college sports event.

✳ ...Eleven percent have played bingo for money.

✳ ...Ten percent have done some riverboat gambling in the past year.

✳ ...Nine percent bet on a horse or dog race in the past year.

✳ ...Fewer than 1 percent have gambled for money on the Internet in the past year.

chapter 6

Coupon Coups

Marketers distributed some 250 billion of them last year, and collectively we redeemed about 5 billion, saving $3.6 billion dollars. Overall, their value keeps rising—and the conditions to redeem them, narrowing. More coupons require us to buy more than one item (22 percent) and more expire earlier (3.1 months on average, down from 10 months a decade ago). More are issued in January than in any other month, followed by October and then May; fewest in December and July. During boom times coupon use dips but rich folks still use them. Do you?

Do you use coupons?

Americans have adopted the habit. Eighty-one percent of us rifle through them in the supermarket. Coupons partially determine what goes in 62 percent of our shopping baskets. On a per capita basis, whites use them more than anyone else (82.6 percent), followed by blacks (76.9 percent). Just 58 percent of both Hispanics and Asians use coupons. Middle-income Americans are likelier than the very rich or very poor to use coupons.

Ever tried to pass off expired coupons?
Almost one in four of us (22.5 percent) has tried to pass off a coupon past its prime.

How much would it take for you to try a different brand of a $2 item?
Seven out of ten of us would need at least a dollar incentive to make the switch, but two in ten wouldn't swap for hyperbolically all the tea in China.

Are you clipping from the Internet?
Fewer than 1 percent of us are "clipping" coupons from the Internet. But experts expect that by 2003 we'll be redeeming more coupons from the Web than from traditional newspaper inserts. Currently, only 23 percent of online users who download a coupon actually redeem it.

> The old-fashioned Sunday-newspaper coupon inserts are the second most read section of the paper after the front page.

Do you use frequent-buyer "punch" cards?
Perhaps it comes with the extra X chromosome—the lure of buying ten and getting one free—but when it comes to punch cards, women are more likely than men to use them for any purpose. Almost one-half of women have used incentive cards, compared with 29 percent of men. Some (48 percent) use it for food—usually the fast variety. A third of American car glove compartments have one for car washes. One-fourth of us go for the volume discount when it comes to oil changes. Only 17 percent use them for video rental and 60 percent for greeting cards. And more than 30 percent of hosiery wearers have used incentive cards to buy tights or stockings. Would you believe that 5 percent of hosiery-card carriers are men?

Are your coupons filed?

Of those of us not too busy raking in the money to worry about husbanding it, just one in five gets a gold star for keeping our coupons current and organized. One-fourth say their storage system is in total shambles.

Would you put an item back on the shelves if you left your coupon for it at home?

More than half of us (57 percent) say we'd forgo the purchase as long as we didn't need the product urgently. Some 2.6 percent would actually go home and retrieve the coupon. Another 2 percent have a more ingenious solution: They'd tell the customer service desk the next time they shopped and present the coupon then.

chapter 7

Just in Case: Insurance

Thirty-five percent of us don't have disability insurance and only 15 percent usually buy travel insurance. Call it gambling when we'll die or hedging your bets if you get sick, but insurance companies have carved a multibillion-dollar business on our willingness to pay "just in case."

Do you have life insurance?

Thirty-eight percent of us have one policy, and 23 percent have two. Eight percent have three, and 24 percent don't have any. The rest aren't telling.

How much coverage do you have?

Just over one-third of us—35 percent—have less than $50,000 in life insurance, just a shade more than those who have shelled out for more than $150,000 in life insurance. Thirteen percent have policies that promise to pay out $50,0000 to $99,999, and 18 percent are in for $100,000 to $149,999.

Have you ever let a life insurance policy lapse?
One-fourth of us have. Another one-third have surrendered one. Our biggest reason for walking: dissatisfaction with the service or policy.

How big a lure is health insurance when choosing a job?
Real big, according to three-fourths of us. Fifty-nine percent of folks surveyed by Consortium Health Plans say they'd even consider looking for a new job if their employer dropped coverage.

> More than one in five adults in this country—44 million—have no private health insurance, sixty-five percent of them because they consider it too expensive or their employer doesn't offer coverage.

Does your company provide it?
Nearly 85 percent of adults with health insurance receive it through their employer or their spouse's.

How much do you kick in for health insurance?
In 2000 employees on average contributed $28 a month for single coverage and $138 for family coverage, vs. $35 and $145 respectively in 1999, according to the Kaiser Family Foundation.

What percentage of your health care costs do you pay?
Employers typically pay 60 to 70 percent of health-care costs, with the employee chipping in 30 to 40 percent.

Have you ever gone without health insurance?
Twenty-four percent have walked this high wire when they were between jobs, and 12 percent claim there was a slight gap in coverage when they left their parents' plan before they found a new umbrella.

Have you ever used COBRA?

One-third of folks have never even heard of COBRA. And fewer than one in five (18.5 percent) have ever availed themselves of this extended insurance coverage for "disengaged" workers.

If you're in an HMO, ever use doctors not in the plan?

Thirty percent of us who belong to an HMO refuse to let the plan dictate whom we see. Thirty-nine percent have switched health care providers so that all their doctors are on the plan.

Are your drugs covered?

More than one-fifth of us—some 45 million Americans—have no prescription drug coverage, and another 32 million consider the coverage they've got inadequate. Thirty-nine million make sacrifices in other parts of our lives to pay for our prescriptions.

Ever bought single-disease insurance ... like against a heart attack?

Either the omens aren't acting up or we're more stoical than hypochondriacal. Only 3.6 percent have purchased single-disease insurance. A good chunk of us—21.7 percent—didn't know you could.

Have you ever appealed a health insurance claim?

More than half of those who have had a medical claim rejected (53.8 percent) say they've requested a reevaluation and followed through to get it. One-third (32.2 percent) have called the insurer to protest but worn out by the process, have given up.

How much time do you spend poring over your health plan?

Not much. Just 17 percent of us spend more than an hour reading our health-plan manuals. Fewer than half give the materials anything more than a cursory glance—until we need to make a claim, and then it's hard to pay attention with all that bile rising.

Are your shrink visits covered?

Some 22 percent of plans cover some sort of mental health care. Most of these have stringent limits.

How about caps, crowns, and whitening and brightening?

Fifty-five percent of all plans provide some dental coverage. Most specify limits and preclude purely cosmetic procedures.

O say, can you see?

Forty-three percent of plans provide some ocular health coverage. But don't rush out for corrective laser vision surgery on our say-so. With most plans, that's money out of your pocket.

How much do you shell out for medicine each year?

The average American spends slightly more than $300 a year on prescription drugs. Amazingly, a good part of those medications are never used. Almost half of people, for example, don't take all the pills in a fourteen-day antibiotic regimen.

Would you rather pay higher premiums for prescription coverage or shell out when you need medicine?

Some 80 percent would rather pay more up front to cover escalating drug costs than be hit with an enormous bill when they need the drugs. That, they figure, would be pouring salt on a wound.

Do you have long-term-care insurance?

Twenty-nine percent of us *say* we have a long-term policy that provides benefits if we're confined at home or in a nursing home due to a medical condition. But in truth less than 1 percent of Americans do. Seventy percent don't know anything about LTC and figure—falsely—that they're covered under their basic health care policy.

Ever asked a doctor to fudge a diagnosis so insurance picks it up?

Seventy-six percent of us wouldn't think of compromising the doctor or embarrassing ourselves by claiming, say, a deviated septum to justify a nose job. Three percent of folks won't say, and 5 percent have no insurance to fudge. Sixteen percent claim they'd try to negotiate coverage in a tactful discussion. Some say they don't have to—that doctors do it automatically.

Some 88 percent of home owners and 23 percent of renters have home insurance. Sixty-eight percent of home buyers say they'd even pay 6 percent more for a new home built to withstand natural disasters.

How much are you paying for auto insurance?

It's about as different as what you and the guy next to you paid for an airline seat. Progressive Auto Insurance says the average difference between the highest and lowest premium for the same driver from different companies is $522 every six months. More than half of us shrug that away, and only 30 percent say they've shopped around to compare auto rates in the past year.

Do you have pet health insurance?

Some 57.3 percent of us have pets but just 1.3 percent have health insurance for Fido. Then again, 3.8 percent didn't even know there was such a thing.

Are you ready for a natural disaster?

Twenty-seven percent say if it hits the fan they'll rely primarily on federal disaster relief.

How do you react to a delayed claims check?

By getting sicker and heavier. People who waited for their insurance claims check for more than one month were four times like-

Two-thirds of men forced to wait more than a month for their claims check said they'd rather spend time with their mother-in-law than with their insurance adjuster.

lier to catch a cold during that time than those who waited less than a month; 16 percent experienced a rise in blood pressure. Twenty-seven percent of women and 14 percent of men who waited for more than a month gained more than five pounds during that time of tense anticipation, while 19 percent of men started smoking cigarettes. People who got reimbursed in less than a month were four times as likely to receive a promotion at work in the following six months compared to people who waited more than six weeks for their claims checks. And 2 percent of couples who received their claims checks in less than two weeks got pregnant in the following four months.

chapter 8

Shelling It Out

William Wordsworth thought the world is too much with us: "Late and soon, getting and spending, we lay waste our powers." A shop-till-you-drop personality like Imelda Marcos might argue that shopping is her power. Where are you in this spectrum?

Which is better: shopping or Prozac?

Shop and spend seems to be the ticket for one-third of us. A Lutheran Brotherhood poll found that 30 percent of us shop when we're feeling low. Women are almost twice as likely as men to find shopping a remedy for what ails them: 38 versus 20 percent.

How about shopping or sex?

For men it's a no-brainer, but more women would actually rather shop till they drop than spend a weekend with a fabulous lover. Half of women say a blank check to shop at a favorite store is their favorite fantasy vs. 18 percent who chose sex with a lover and 15 percent who opted for a fountain of youth.

What do you like to buy?

Forget shoes and jewelry. Thirty-five percent say their favorite purchases are things for their homes, 25 percent say travel and entertainment, and 16 percent say investments.

A keepsake or a memory: which would you rather buy?

Seventy-nine percent of us would rather buy an expensive item that we could keep for a long time than splurge on an experience.

Although 73 percent of us say that buying something makes us happy, it trails grabbing the phone, turning on the TV, getting together with friends, and even spring cleaning as a way to chase the blues. It's also behind praying, reading, eating, and bathing but edges out cooking and working out.

How often do you shop for food?

If you've got a family, counting the big usually-once-a-week trip to the supermarket and other dock-ins, you average 3.5 shopping trips a week. Younger people actually shop more.

How much time do you spend in the supermarket?

Believe it or not, the average shopper spends only twenty-one minutes buying groceries and covers only 23 percent of the store during each drop-in, according to a study by Frito-Lay.

Do you pay attention to unit pricing?

Two-thirds of us pay acute attention to unit pricing in the supermarket—or at least claim to. Twenty-five percent don't give a hoot, and 8.7 percent wonder what unit pricing really means.

Do you take the free samples offered ... to avoid buying lunch?

Sixty percent of us take the freebie demonstration foods served up in the supermarket. On average, 37 percent wind up purchasing what they've just sampled.

Do you head to the store with a list?

Three-quarters of men (77 percent) and even more women (84 percent) regularly arm themselves with shopping lists before heading into a supermarket. But research shows they're just as likely to make spontaneous purchases as those without lists.

Some 52 percent read a magazine while standing in line and then put it back before the cashier rings it up. (That's also why, when we do buy, three-fourths of us reach behind or under for a fresher copy.)

Do you often buy more than you intended?

Robert Burns knew shopping behavior when he said the best-laid plans often get waylaid. Ninety-three percent of us claim that even with elaborate preparation, we still buy more than what we'd originally intended when we set out. In fact, 59 percent of all supermarket merchandise is bought on impulse. The stuff flanking the cashier includes the most frequently purchased impulse items.

Do you buy store brands or pricier national ones?

Eighty-five percent swear they can tell the difference between Heinz and wanna-be ketchups. Only 15 percent stock up on store brands to save a few cents. But whether we do often depends on how far from our mouth the item goes. Plastic garbage bags, OK. Pickles? Forget it.

Would you buy a different brand if it supported a cause you love?
Two-thirds of us would, assuming, of course, that the brand we're considering is the same price as the brand it's replacing.

Now for the good stuff: When do you start your holiday shopping?
Twenty-two percent of men and 9 percent of women leave the gift buying to the last minute—or more accurately, to the day or two before. Another 12 percent start stocking up with the January sales—eleven months before! But for half of us, Thanksgiving signals the start of the shopping season. Start and finish are two different things, however. Fifteen percent of adults are usually still shopping for gifts after 6 P.M. Christmas Eve.

Almost 90 percent of people who own pets put a little something under the tree for Fido.

Do you usually buy unplanned gifts?
Youth may be lost on the young, but spontaneity seems to fade with age. One-third of young adults almost always wind up buying something if they want it—more than double the proportion of 55-to-64-year-olds who snap to the occasion. Forty-three percent of people tend to go overboard on holiday gifts.

Do you set limits for holiday gifts?
Fifty-seven percent of us head to the mall with a preconceived amount—although few stick to those limits religiously.

Are you peeved if someone exchanges your gift?
Twenty percent admit they'd be steamed about it.

Do you know the size of the person you're shopping for?
Most women know the collar and inseam size of the men they plan

to gift, but only about half of men head to the stores knowing the difference between a size two and a size twelve.

Do you wrap your own gifts or pay to have them wrapped?
Twenty-two percent have someone else do the wrapping and consider it money well spent.

How much do you expect to spend this holiday season?
Just before the 2000 countdown, shoppers expected to shell out $1,684 during the holiday season, according to American Express. The National Retail Federation estimates that we'll spend, on average, $836 of that for gifts.

Whatcha gonna buy?
Usually what you yourself would want. That translates into clothes: Sixty percent of

Nearly three out of every four men (72 percent) say they'd gladly fork over up to $25 to have someone else deal with holiday shopping. Twenty percent would shell out as much as $50, and another 7 percent would hand over more.

people say that's their top holiday gift. Other big hits: music, tapes, CDs, and movies (42 percent); toys and games (37 percent); good reads (35 percent); electronics and appliances (33 percent); good scents (31 percent); and home furnishings (24 percent).

How much will you spend on that special someone?
Most shoppers splurge on one person: Nearly 40 percent will spend an average of $669.

Do you bottom feed right after the holidays?
Twenty-nine percent shop for gifts right after Christmas.

Are you often caught off guard by what you've spent?
Nearly all of us claim to be aware of what we spend each month. But 18 percent of the indulgers surveyed said they usually have trouble paying the bills when the damage is totaled up.

Ever buy on layaway?
Two-thirds of us (68 percent) have never done so.

How much does your household spend in a year?
The average family spends on average $15,210 a year for day-to-day and household expenses, such as groceries, gas, fast food, and cell phone and Internet service. Throw in another $19,232 for rent, car payments, property taxes, and other living expenses, reports American Express.

How much do you spend...

✳ **...To keep Fluffy and Duke healthy?**
The average human companion shells out $173 a year on supplements and vet visits for his animal companion.

✳ **...On computer gear and the phone?**
About $211 on computer hardware, software, and online services for pleasure, and $909 on telephone equipment and services.

✳ **...To get around and chow down?**
Food at home sets us back an average of $54 per person per week—with food away from home adding another $33. To get around: an average of about $500 a month.

✳ **...Dressing to kill?**
We spend around $142 a month on clothes and accessories—5 percent of our collective total expenditures.

How much do you spend on doctor visits?
The average person spent $906 at the doctor's in 2000. Estimates are that will top $1,170 in 2005. It was $583 in 1990 and $739 in 1995.

Do you shop around for prescription drugs?
We may comparison shop on virtually everything else, but when it comes to drugs, 45.5 percent pay whatever is asked because we trust our pharmacy.

If given an extra $500, what part would you spend on clothes?
Women would spend $278 and men $202.

Have you ever had clothes custom-made?
Only 35 percent have ever had apparel made just for them. Six percent of us do so regularly.

How much does it cost to gimme shelter?
A third of our budget goes to providing a roof over our heads. Home owners spend around $1.50 for every $1 renters spend on housing, averaging just over $900 a month versus $630 for renters.

What do you typically spend on a Valentine's Day gift?
It seems men are the ones from Venus. On average, they spend $107; women, on average, shell out just $46.

When do you usually do your back-to-school shopping?
If you wait until Labor Day, chances are there won't be much left on the shelves. Three out of four students and parents have finished the task by mid-August.

Do you use the Internet to avoid sales tax?
Only 5 percent of us have.

Ever canceled an online purchase because of shipping fees?

Sixty-three percent of us have hesitated to complete the checkout once we see what the delivery charges add to the order. One out of five shoppers (21 percent) has kept something he or she didn't want because the shipping fees to return it were so steep.

What one luxury would you spend money on this year?

One in five of us would opt for a butler or maid, while almost as many (18 percent) would shell out to sleep as comfortably and as long as they wanted. Thirteen percent would indulge in a personal trainer, and 11 percent in a chauffeur and limousine. Seven percent would spend on a full-time cook, and 3 percent on a face-lift.

Ever bought counterfeit goods, like a "Gucci" handbag on the street?

That only reinforces thievery—and besides, they're obvious copies. Perhaps that's why 67.5 percent pass them by. Four percent found the pricing irresistible and have tried to pass off the clone as an original. Another 28 percent bought without deluding themselves about the item's authenticity. One percent were surprised they aren't real.

Do you budget for holiday spending?

Not likely. American Bankers Association found that 65 percent of us usually make no budget for holiday spending. Twenty percent of all consumer purchases are made in the final months of the year. Most of us overspend on holidays by nearly $100 more than we think.

How long does it usually take to pay off holiday debts?

People imagine they can be free and clear in three months, but it's usually six months later before they've paid off those bills.

How many holiday gifts do you usually buy for your children?
Two-thirds of us buy more than we can count. Some 3.6 percent buy sixteen to twenty presents (including stocking stuffers), and 4 percent wrap up eleven to fifteen gifts. Just over 11 percent buy six to ten gifts, and 12 percent between one and five.

How do you feel about giving a gift certificate?
Half of us love their convenience. But 27.3 percent avoid them because it would be obvious what was spent. Another 22.4 percent feel uncomfortable about being so exposed but buy them anyway.

What do you do with unwanted gifts?
Some 31 percent keep them and try to use them—wearing that five-inch-wide giraffe tie to an intimate dinner for two ... at home, say. Thirty percent tuck them away, and 13 percent toss them in the trash. Six percent bring them back to the store for cash.

Do you consider shopping fun?
More than likely that depends on whether you've got the Y chromosome: 79 percent of women like to shop, while 74 percent of men try to avoid it.

chapter 9

Stashing It Away

We all know that a penny saved is lots more than a penny earned, but the truth is, not all that many of us are socking it away regularly. A lot claim that they've got all they can do just to meet the bills and that the future will take care of itself. How disciplined are you?

Got a cash cushion to break a financial fall?
Only 52 percent of us have money saved up outside of a work-related savings or retirement plan. Nearly one-fifth of folks earning more than $50,000 a year have nothing saved.

Got the green to cover a pink slip?
Half of us (54 percent) would fall behind on bills within three months if we lost our jobs. Twenty-six percent would fall behind immediately, while 28 percent would be up the creek within three months.

How much do you sock away?
If you're an average Joe, you sock away 4.9 percent of your net

income into all savings and investments, the U.S. Department of Commerce found. That's about half the 10 percent savings rate experts recommend. The U.S. Department of Education says we *think* we're stashing away an average of 15 percent. One-fifth of us admit they wouldn't even come close to estimating how much money they've got socked away.

Ever use a bank's Christmas Club account?
That went out with refrigerators that needed defrosting, according to three-fourths of us. Just 11 percent have ever used one.

Still own savings bonds?
Call it bondage: One in three families today still own U.S. savings bonds—the kind Grandma used to buy each birthday. Collectively, that's worth $5 billion not yet redeemed.

Do you save the max in your company's 401(k) plan?
Only 14 percent of participants contribute all they can.

Did you contribute to an IRA last year?
Only 18 percent of workers contributed to an IRA last year.

Nineteen percent stash their emergency funds in a piggy bank, especially one that doesn't open. Three percent say they keep a few thousand dollars hidden at home.

Ever borrow against your 401(k) plan?
More than two-thirds hold their 401(k) sacred, but the rest have dipped into it to cover special purchases.

How much did you have saved before you started investing?
Maybe in the old days you socked some away before taking the plunge, but no more. Thirty-five percent of investors had virtually

no money stashed away before plunging into the stock market. Twenty-six percent had three months' salary, and 16 percent, six months' worth tucked away. Twenty-three percent had a comfortable year's cache in the bank.

chapter 10

Blankety Bank

Although 10 million of us don't have checking accounts, when it comes to saving forget about the mattress or kitchen freezer. We may stow a few bills there, but when it comes to partners in managing our money, banks win hands down.

We know you love your bank, but how often do you visit it?
More folks usually go to the bank once a week than any other frequency (35 percent). Some 27 percent usually drop in two to three times a week, and 25 percent stop by every ten days to two weeks. But 8.4 percent rarely go there while 3.6 percent claim they make a deposit or withdrawal daily.

With how many banks do you have concurrent relationships?
Almost half of us—44 percent—are serial monogamists. Some 37.5 percent are two-timers, while 12.7 percent maintain concurrent relationships with three banks. Almost 5 percent have dealings with four or more banks.

When did you open your very first checking account?
On average, for both men and women by the time they were twenty.

Do you order checks from your bank or get them elsewhere for less?
Banks know the secret: Don't ask, and few will think to ask them. It's called automatic renewal, and 56.2 percent of us fall for it—saying our checks (and the deductions for them) arrive automatically. An enterprising 28 percent go elsewhere because it's cheaper.

Are your personal checks identity badges?
Forget the graphics. Few of us consider our checks a badge of status like a car or wristwatch. With checks, plain vanilla reigns. Eighty-four percent want them simple and unadorned. But 12 percent prefer checks with sunsets on them. Another 2.2 percent opt to have them festooned with kittens or other cute animals, and 2 percent go for angels on their checks. Current Inc. of Colorado, says that the most popular design is still "safety" blue.

We write, on average, just over twenty checks a month.

Is your address on your checks?
Three-fourths of us include our address on the check.

Ever bounced a check or received an overdraft slip?
Twenty-seven percent of us have bounced a check—embarrassing and costly. In the year 2000, the national average fee for a bounced check came to $23.87, up from $21.75 in 1998, according to bankrate.com. And 41.5 percent have received an overdraft slip from the postman.

Know how much you've got in the bank?
Most of us could say to a few cents what our current balance is.

Eighty-one percent claim to even know the amount of our credit card balances.

Ever stopped a check?
Twenty-two percent have done so once, while 12 percent have the drill down pat from doing it more often.

Do you balance your checkbook against your account statement?
More than half of us with checking accounts—56.7 percent—consider this akin to breathing, a preordained, automatic ritual. Alas, almost one-third of us—31.9 percent—struggle to get to it but slip up for lack of time. The rest delegate it to the bank—and are prepared to suffer whatever consequences that accounting produces.

How often do you balance your checkbook?
Ninety-four percent do so at least once a month.

How often do you use an ATM?
Most do so once or twice a week or 6.2 visits a month.

Do you secretly prefer visiting a teller to using an ATM?
For all the interest in face-to-face contact, by an eight-to-one margin, we'd rather use an automated machine than a real live teller, with Gen Xers most likely to prefer to swipe their cards rather than talk to a teller.

How much do you typically withdraw?
No need to load up. Almost half of us—48 percent—usually take out $60 or less per visit. Twenty-eight percent typically extract $100, while 13.3 percent usually go for $200. Eleven percent usually withdraw $250 or more.

Ever lost an ATM card?
Fewer than one in five of us has ever lost our ATM card.

Ever withdraw from a bank where you have no account?

More than half of us—58 percent—have done so, and forty-one percent feel the convenience is worth the surcharge. Almost 6 percent did so once, and then they saw what the bank charged them for the courtesy. Non-account-holder ATM withdrawals cost an average of $1.35 a shot.

Do you use direct deposit?

Virtually all Germans, Japanese, and Canadians have their companies deposit their paychecks directly, but only 56.2 percent of American workers do, according to the National Automated Clearing House Association. But 95 percent of government employees and 69 percent of Social Security recipients use it.

When did you open your first savings account?

Sixteen seems to be the magic age. Forty-three percent of men and 31 percent of women opened savings accounts then.

Ever go to a check-cashing center?

Only 8.6 percent have ever used those services and even fewer of the well-heeled.

Ever get a certified check?

Two-thirds of us have but 6 percent don't even know what it is.

Ever sent a money order?

They're not extinct after all: 58.6 percent have sent one.

Do you pay your bank—or does your bank pay you?

Three-fourths of us don't pay anything for banking services and instead just sit back and collect interest. Those who have to pay to maintain an account shell out on average less than $3 a month.

Whatcha making on your interest-bearing account?
Well, at least you're not paying it. The average checking account pays $23 in interest over the year and requires a minimum of $662.51 to open.

Do you bank over your computer?
In early 2000 just under 5 million of us were. But that's expected to more than double by 2002.

How much time do you spend waiting in line at the bank?
We spend on average half a week a year waiting at the bank, a fraction of what we wait for tech support or wireless customer service.

How often do you hear from your banker?
Sadly, the days of Mr. Jones greeting you as you step into Central Bank on Main Street are for reminiscing only. Only 8 percent of people claim their banker checks in periodically to see how they and their finances are doing. Thirty-seven percent don't even know they have a banker. And 18 percent hear from their banker whenever the institution has a new fee-paying service they want to sell.

How often does your bank mess up on something?
For all the abuse banks take, it seems they actually do a pretty good job. Almost half of us—47.4 percent—can't recall any screw-ups.

chapter 11

Little Green Lies

What's the relationship between money and ethics? Is it Lady MacBeth or Jiminy Cricket? Would you try to get away with whatever you could for financial gain if you knew you wouldn't get caught?

Do you lie about money?

Of course we lie about money. One in four admits to fibbing about what they earn, far fewer than those who lie about their weight.

Ever tried to pad an insurance bill to cover the deductible?

Four out of ten of us have tried to inflate the bill. Women, especially middle-aged ones, are least likely to submit an accurate bill. More often than not, they go through unquestioned.

Ever bought something intending to wear and then return it?

Astonishingly, almost one in ten of us has purchased something we intend to wear once and then return. More amazing, perhaps:

Most don't feel much guilt about it. Almost three times as many younger people as older ones admit they've borrowed an article of clothing for a one-time fling.

Ever switched tags to pay less in the store?
One in ten of us has engaged in this sort of theft with under-35-year-olds and those earning less than $40,000 much more likely to do so.

Think you've ever been deceived by a financial services rep?
Thirty-eight percent of the workers interviewed at U.S. financial services firms say they have personally witnessed co-employees lying to or misleading customers.

Ever used someone else's credit card ... or had your own used?
Chances are, if you've been involved with credit card fraud, it happened online. According to Gartner Group, just over 1 percent of all online purchases are fraudulent. In the offline world, only 0.06 percent to 0.09 percent of purchases are bogus. That means credit card fraud on the Internet is twelve times higher than at bricks-and-mortar stores. Indeed, 64 percent of all charge-backs, where consumers are credited for charges made on their cards, for online purchases are the result of fraud, while only 44 percent of charge-backs for offline transactions are shady.

If a waiter forgot to charge for something, would you point it out?
Not likely. A survey by ICR Research Group found that 24 percent of diners wouldn't correct a waiter who undercharged them.

Ever sneaked into a show to avoid buying a ticket?
Nineteen percent have made reverse use of the theater's exit door.

If a broker could make you extra money by giving you preferential treatment over others, would you give him your business?
Nearly two out of five (39 percent) would willingly use a shady commodity broker to score some extra bucks.

If you found a wallet with money and ID in it, what would you do?
Nine percent admit they'd keep the cash if it were $100, while 13 percent would look the other way for $1,000 in a wallet.

Would you commit a crime for $10 million if you knew you wouldn't get caught?
Almost one-quarter of us (23 percent) would go criminal for that kind of loot, but men are almost twice as likely as women to go for it. Lower the booty to $100,000, and 8 percent would still do it.

Would you marry someone you didn't love for money?
Seven percent of people admit that given the chance—and the size of the mine—they'd gold dig. Nine percent of wealthy people say they'd align for money, versus just 2 percent of those who earn less than $25,000.

Ever knowingly left a store without paying for something?
Twenty-nine percent of people admit they've strolled out of a store without paying for something intentionally. One-fourth of those who shoplifted once say that rather than frighten or morally repel them, the shoplifting experience heightened their interest. The average value of merchandise stolen per visit: $56.67.

Ever smuggled candy into a movie to avoid paying high prices?
More than half of us—53.7 percent—have done so and think it's justified, considering how jacked up the concessionaire's prices are. Ten percent have done so but see it as cheating.

Ever fibbed about age to take advantage of a discount?
Seventy percent say no way, although there are an awful lot of old-looking teens getting children's tickets at the movies. Some 22 percent forget how old they really are only when the price differential is compelling.

If an ATM gave you too much money, what would you do?
"Finders keepers, losers weepers" say one-third of us. But 44.9 percent claim they'd get it back to the bank as fast as possible. Seven percent expect they'd do nothing except worry about it.

Ever not listed a preexisting condition to get a better health insurance deal?
Eight percent have done so but two-thirds worry that if the insurance company found out they'd be left high and dry.

Ever not listed a young driver on an auto insurance policy?
Eight percent have and 11 percent would if they were sure they could get away with it, but 81 percent worry their insurance would be worthless if the company found out.

Do you always declare everything you bought overseas to U.S. Customs?
Almost two-thirds of us—63 percent—claim to always declare the truth, even if it's more than $400 worth of goods exempt from duty. But one in four tries to pretend that she already owned that snazzy alligator bag before heading to Madrid.

chapter 12

Bills, Bills, Bills

Whether they come in e-form or traditional p- (postal) form, bills are a nasty fact of life. But it's how we respond to them that separates the wheat from the chaff. Credit card bills are the one we hate the most, followed by car loan and auto insurance bills.

Who pays the bills?

More women (72 percent) than men (52 percent) handle the bill paying at home, American Express reports.

How much time do you spend paying bills?

The average family spends six hours a month on this. Gals are almost twice as likely as guys (59 percent versus 32 percent) to scrutinize the bills before paying them.

Check or card?

Despite all the talk that plastic is ubiquitous, 83 percent of people pay with checks. Only 9 percent never use checks to pay their bills.

Do you pay your bills on time?

No, it's not the postal service. Nearly half (45 percent) of bill payers admit that they're sometimes late. Thirty-two percent routinely procrastinate.

How about online?

Only 4.5 percent of us have paid at least one bill online, but estimates are that number will mushroom in the next few years. Currently, fewer than 1 percent of bills are distributed electronically so most bills paid online are still received offline. Sixty-nine percent are too nervous about security to pay bills online while 60 percent think they'll be subject to fees. And 44 percent question the recourse they'd have if they made a mistake.

chapter 13

Where's That Receipt?

ome say you are what you eat. We believe you are what you
keep—that the secret of your personality lies in the chaos
or order of your financial records. Are you a pack rat or an
ascetic?

Are your financial records well organized?
That's one (perhaps the only) benefit of tax time. More than half
of us (57.4 percent) say the April deadline is impetus to get ship-
shape. Another 30.5 percent claim their documentation is all
there but too Herculean to get precise. Twelve percent admit
defeat.

Where do you stash documents?
Two-thirds of us (67.9 percent) use a filing cabinet. Another 9.5
percent use a home safe. Almost as many (8.8 percent) stow documents in a bank safe-deposit box, while 4 percent find the kitchen
drawer just fine. The rest have some other ingenious storage
place—including the trash bin.

When do you file bills, credit card receipts, et al.?
Forty-one percent of us deal with them as soon as we receive them. Another 36 percent attack the pile once a month and 18 percent once in a blue moon.

Where is your automobile title?
No, it's not the mark of genius, but 17.3 percent of us admit we keep it in the glove compartment. Three-fourths (75.4 percent) stow it safely in the house, but 7.3 percent have no idea where it is.

Do you keep receipts for valuable items like jewelry and furniture?
Just over half of us (54 percent) do so religiously, while another one-third document the purchase only if they anticipate a problem. Another 8.7 percent are waylaid by their own disorganization, while 3.9 percent consider life too short to bother with it.

How do you discard credit card receipts and other account info?
Thirty-four percent of us use a paper shredder, and 40.5 percent manually cut up and disfigure account information before throwing it away. Seven percent burn receipts. Only 18.3 percent toss them away unaltered.

Do you keep financial records on your computer?
Forty-three percent of us do.

Do you have a bank safe-deposit box?
One in four of us (26 percent) has one now but 58.7 percent have never rented one.

Do you keep any share certificates at home?
Over 90 percent of investors have share certificates for at least some of their holdings tucked away in a bottom drawer.

Do you usually send in product warranty cards?
Although it only takes a moment, doesn't cost a dime (most come postage paid), and could potentially save us a lot of dough, 39 percent of men and 32 percent of women almost never mail in warranty cards. Two-thirds of those forty-five and older comply, perhaps knowing from experience that things go wrong.

How long do you keep:

... Canceled checks?
Two out of three of us keep them for years. Twelve percent toss them after a year, and another 12.3 percent keep them for just a few months. Twenty percent of folks don't keep them at all.

... Pay stubs?
Almost 53 percent keep them indefinitely while 14.7 percent toss them right away.

... ATM receipts?
Sixteen percent throw them out as soon as they leave the cash machine while 45.9 percent reconcile them with their bank statement and 4.6 percent hold them until they file their taxes.

... Home mortgage statements?
More than half of us (51.4 percent) keep them for as long as we own our homes. Eight percent keep them only until the mortgage company receives payment, and 11 percent do an annual cleanup. Almost one-third—29.4 percent—hold on to them forever.

... Monthly bank or mutual fund statements?
More than half (59.8 percent) of us keep them ad infinitum. Twenty percent toss them only when they get a year-end summary statement. Some 4.7 percent discard the statement as soon as it arrives. Another 15.4 percent wait for inspiration and toss randomly.

chapter 14

Rolling in Dough

Millions of mothers have told their daughters that it's as easy to love a rich man as a poor one. But how do you define rich today, and how much do we want to be it? To what lengths will we go for real money?

How much does it take to be "rich" today?

In the old days—1984—28 percent of us would have felt like kings with $100,000 in savings. Now a mere 2 percent consider that wealth. Four percent consider $250,000 in the bank rich; sixteen years earlier, 11 percent did. Similarly, while 17 percent considered $500,000 real money back then, today only 7 percent do. Even $1 million doesn't cut it any more. Only 25 percent of us consider that rich, while 28 percent say they'd need $3 million to feel affluent— the same number who define rich as a minimum of $5 million.

Do you expect to strike it rich?

Optimism reigns. More than half of all college students expect to be millionaires by age forty. One in four expect to make their first million by thirty. Just 29 percent don't ever expect to make a million.

Have you ever bought a program that promised to make you rich?
Fewer than 1 in 100 of us actually has subscribed to such a program but almost 1 in 10 has at least fleetingly contemplated doing so.

Would you rather be really rich or score in other areas?
One in four of us would rather have the money than family bliss. Only 7.8 percent would rather find the love of their lives, and 2.2 percent win the Nobel Peace Prize. Just 3 percent would choose eternal youth instead.

> Money, it seems, is more practical than celebrity. Three out of five admit they'd rather win the lottery than an Oscar, Grammy, or Nobel Peace Prize.

Are you secretly wary of wealth?
Lots of us, though fascinated by newly minted game-show millionaires, are suspicious of the moral effects of money. More than 80 percent believe that having lots of money makes people greedy and stuck-up. Three out of four think the rich are insensitive. One in three insist they would not want to be wealthy.

If you had more money than you knew what to do with, what would you do with it?
Seventy-one percent would use it to live as they chose. Fifty-eight percent would spend it to add excitement and dazzle to their humdrum lives. And 56 percent say they'd use the dough to reduce stress.

Long-lost Uncle Charles leaves you a grand inheritance of $10 million. How would that change where you live?
Fifty-eight percent would continue living as we had before the sudden largesse. Forty-five percent would move nearby, while 22 per-

cent would move far away. Forty-eight percent would buy a second or even a third home, and 52 percent would pour some of the loot into improving their current home.

Your lucky number just came in: Would you quit your job?

If we came into $10 million, 42 percent of us would keep on truckin' at the same old job. Twenty-two percent would start a business. Another 10 percent would change jobs or fields. Westerners are more than twice as likely as Northeasterners to want to strike off on their own (15 percent versus 6 percent).

Would the windfall affect the time you spend with your family?

Three-fourths of us expect we'd spend more time with our families. But 5 percent figure a ton of cash would mean they'd spend less time with their offspring because they'd hire help. Seven percent would also "buy" some time away from their partners.

Would this sudden wealth change your love life?

Ring those wedding bells. If fortune fell on them, 16 percent of folks would marry or remarry their partner. Yet 3 percent would use the manna to unravel their alliance. For them, money may not buy love, but it can certainly buy more space.

How much would it take to significantly change your life?

Nine percent would need more than $10 million to significantly change our lives, whereas an extra $100,000 would dramatically change things for one-third of us. Thirty percent would find things shaken up for $100,000 to $1 million, while 23.8 percent calculate it would require $1 million to $10 million to turn things around.

What would be your first purchase?

One in four would buy a new car or home or take off on vacation.

Thirteen percent would buy a new home for other family members. Eleven percent would immediately hire an attorney.

How would you spend a $10,000 windfall?
More than one-third of us would pay off loans and credit-card bills; 1 percent would use the windfall to splurge on themselves.

How much, if any, of a $10 million gift would you give to charity?
Twenty-seven percent—misers—wouldn't give a dime, while 21 percent would give away half. Twenty-eight percent would donate $50,000, and 21 percent would tithe a tenth.

How would this windfall change you as a person?
Two-thirds imagine they'd still be the same sweet, lovable old Joe. Sixteen percent fantasize that they would be happier, and 12 percent imagine it would turn them into a "typical rich snob." One percent expect it would up their misery index.

chapter 15

What You'd Do for Money

Money talks and motivates. Hands down, the best incentive to get action is cash. Nine out of ten prefer it to miles, points, and other frills in rewards programs. So how far would you go for it?

Would you walk on the wild side for a big payout?

Generally (and legally) speaking, 73 percent of us say we'd take risks to reap rewards, although 55 percent of those say the payouts have got to be big-time to interest them.

Would you live on a deserted island for a year for $1 million?

Sixty-five percent would do the Robinson Crusoe thing for $1 million.

Would you kiss a stranger for $200?

One-third of us (32 percent) might even plant a smooch on a frog for that quick cash. Another one-third say that to overcome their shyness or aversion they'd need at least $500, but 37 percent wouldn't be interested.

How about the frog for $50?

Three out of four people say they'd do it.

For $2,500, would you eat a healthy but restricted diet for a year—forfeiting all of the money if you snacked?

Three out of five of us find that inducement too great to pass up.

How about wear the same underwear for a week for $500?

Sixty-one percent of folks say it's a deal if they could wash themselves. Forty-eight percent would go two full weeks sans bath or shower for $2,500.

Would you go up against a heavyweight boxing champ for $100,000?

Only one in five of us would take the punches for the dough.

Would you swallow a worm for $300 if it wouldn't make you sick?

Twenty-one percent would do it for $300, but 26 percent would need at least $1,000. Forty-seven percent wouldn't for all the tea in China.

Would you serve six months in jail for someone else for a cool million bucks?

Prison is pretty uninviting. Only 30 percent of us would take the rap for someone else in a medium-security jail.

Would you dress more revealingly to double your salary?

Unscrupulous sellout or not, just 47.5 percent would hike up our skirts and show some cleavage if it meant doubling our pay.

Would you keep a job you hated for big bucks?

Twenty-three percent say they would hold their nose and collect the cash for a short time at least. Ten percent wouldn't take this Faustian bargain for a minute. Seven percent confess that they are already doing it.

> Fifteen out of 100 people would undergo having an irreversible sex change for an endless allowance.

How about take a three-month vow of silence for $20,000?

Two-thirds of us would button up assuming we could write our thoughts and listen to others. A third doubt they'd have the resolve to remain mute that long.

How much would you pay to be stress free?

Everyone complains about stress, but 55 percent would not fork over even $50 a month to be guaranteed to be worry free.

Would you sleep on the street, beggar style, for a week for $2,000?

Fifty-eight percent of people feel that's a fair deal.

Would you cut in front of an old woman on line for $100?

Two-thirds of us think it's too much like attacking Mom. Our collective reluctance rises to 78 percent if we know the potential victim.

For $10,000, would you shave your head?

Fifty-nine percent would do it in a heartbeat. Some don't have to; they're already there.

For $3,000, would you reveal a deep, dark secret you promised your best friend you'd hold sacred?

Sixty-four percent of confidantes believe in the blood oath and insist they'd take that secret to the grave. Twenty-four percent anticipate they'd spill the beans for the cash.

How far would you go for $10 million?

The truth is, most of us would do just about anything. One-quarter would abandon all their friends and church, or become a prostitute for a week, or change their race or sex. And 7 percent—one out of every fourteen of us—would even murder for that amount. Astonishingly, most of us would do all of this for as little as $3 million—but not $2 million. Go figure.

Would you spy for another country for a lot of money?

Not on your life, say 75 percent of us. Fifteen percent would consider it, depending on how big the payoff was and if they could get away with it. Five percent would be influenced by their own neediness. The rest won't decide ahead of time and figure they'll never have to.

Would you have sex for money?

Sixty percent of us dismiss the idea flat out, but 6.7 percent think getting paid for something they enjoy is a good deal, and 20.4 percent say it depends on who with.

Would you pose nude in a magazine for money?

Nope, say half of us. Just 11.7 percent say why not? For the rest, it depends on the amount of money proffered and their own need for it.

chapter 16

Plastic

I*f neither Hamlet nor Laertes heeded Polonius's advice, why should we? The "Neither a borrower nor a lender be" bromide seems to have fallen into disuse in twenty-first-century America, where the national debt reflects our personal balance sheets. How do you stack up?*

Where are you on the debt horizon?

Seventeen percent of Americans are in the hole, deep in debt with little hope of clambering out. Twenty percent describe their financial position as precarious. Forty percent take on debt but claim to always pay up on time, and 23 percent crow that they are debt free. Collectively, we owe more than $1.266 trillion in nonmortgage debt—roughly $5,000 for every American.

Do you have a credit card?

Nowadays, almost as many people carry credit cards as have a driver's license. Three times as many have them as have valid passports. Just 9 percent of Americans have none. The average card carrier has three or four bank cards and eight to ten credit cards.

And 23 percent of American households now have at least one debit card.

How often do you use them?
Seventy percent use their credit cards fewer than five times a month; 20 percent use them between five and ten times a month; and 10 percent use them more than ten times a month.

How much debt are you carrying on your credit cards?
The average credit card carries an outstanding debt of $2,287.

Do you pay your monthly credit card balance in full?
Almost half of us (49 percent) always pay our credit card balance in full, thus avoiding any interest charges. But 5 percent usually pay only the minimum payment, and another 10 percent pay what they can afford at the moment.

Do you usually pay off loans early?
Sixty percent of us usually pay off any loans early, while for 9 percent, it depends on who did the lending: Borrowers tend to take more latitude if the money is from family or friends.

What was your first loan application for?
For 44 percent of us it was a personal loan, and for 27 percent, a home loan. Sixteen percent lost their loan virginity on an auto loan, and the rest for various other ends including college.

Ever had your credit card authorization denied?
Thirty percent of us have suffered through this indignity.

When did you get your first card?
Women, on average, got their first credit card at 25.7 years—four months later than men, on average, received theirs.

Ever obtained your credit record, and was it correct?
Just over half of us have gone to the trouble. Half of those who did found mistakes on them. The Federal Trade Commission says it receives more complaints about credit reporting than about any other issue.

How many credit card invitations land in your mailbox each month?
Nearly three-fourths of us receive at least one a month. Four billion are sent out each year. The average household receives forty-three. Almost all of us (98.6 percent) throw them away unread. But that still leaves six hot prospects for every four hundred sent.

What will get you to try a new card?
Most of us have all the cards we need, thank you. But if we were to seek another, the most attractive benefit would be a cash rebate, cited by 31 percent. A discount or credit toward a store purchase is the next most desirable incentive, at 22 percent. Only 20 percent of potential customers are interested in frequent flier miles.

Some 19.2 million adults have bought something online with their cards. More than half use a Visa card. One-third use MasterCard, and 15 percent use American Express.

How about student debt?
About 75 percent of undergraduates now carry credit cards—with an average balance of $1,843.

How spooked are you at using your credit card online?
Releasing personal information online is a real spine-tingler: More than 80 percent of us say that someone misusing our personal information online is more likely to make our heads spin

like Linda Blair's in *The Exorcist* than running into a group of ghosts. Women are more spooked here than men, 36 percent to 28 percent.

What kinds of cards do you have on you?

Eighty-nine percent of us carry around a credit card, and 61 percent an ATM card. Fifty-nine percent tote around membership cards. Thirty-seven percent carry debit cards linked to checking accounts, while 33 percent carry prepaid cards primarily for phone usage, 25 percent loyalty cards, and 4 percent smart cards.

> Some 35.5 percent of us have cut up our charge cards to avoid temptation.

How much interest do you pay a year?

We shell out on average $400 per household.

Got a home mortgage?

Collectively, we owe $4.5 trillion in home mortgages, up from $2.5 trillion a decade ago.

Ever been denied credit?

One in five of us, especially younger folks, has been denied credit. A Freddie Mac report, based on a survey of 12,000 households with incomes of less than $75,000, showed that 48 percent of African Americans and 34 percent of Hispanics had poor credit histories, compared to 27 percent of whites.

How many credit transactions do you make each month?

On average, we sign 12.8 credit and 11.1 debit card transactions a month.

Ever ask for cash back when buying something with a card?
Only one in three of us has ever done so.

Do you charge tabs under, say, $20?
It's the thing to do! Fifty-four percent of us say it's acceptable to use cards for receipts under $20, compared with 45 percent of those surveyed a year earlier.

Do you use your credit card to buy groceries? Gas?
Thirty-six percent usually pay for food with a card, and 60 percent of motorists pay for their gasoline with cash.

Ever had the misfortune of a lost or stolen credit card?
Some 23.9 percent of us say we've lost one, and 9.57 percent say they've had one stolen.

Do you pay tuition with a credit card?
Nineteen percent do and count all the frequency miles as a side benefit. Another 23.7 percent decided not to because the school adds a service charge.

Do you buy stock with a credit card?
Just 3 percent of us have ever bought stocks with a credit card.

Do you spend more when you use a credit card?
One-third of us can't prove it for sure but suspect that we do.

Ever raised the spending limits on your credit card?
Half of us have done so at least once.

Ever been contacted by a collection agent for a late bill?
Twenty-three percent of us have experienced this jolt.

Ever consolidate your debt?
Two out of five of us—41.2 percent—have consolidated debt.

Ever filed for personal bankruptcy?
Big surprise here: Even while prosperity reigned, more people than ever were declaring bankruptcy. They've been filing for protection from creditors at the rate of more than 1 million a year since 1996, up fourfold since 1979. Some 2 percent of us have at one point in our lives filed for bankruptcy.

Ever been the creditor in a bankruptcy?
Eighteen percent of us have been left holding the bag. Thirty-nine percent have pursued settlement, even taking it to court, while 13.9 percent let the matter lapse early in the game.

Why did you fall into debt?
More than half of those in debt—52 percent—blame their predicament on poor money management. The rest say a "life event" such as a divorce or medical problem propelled them into the red.

Ever seek help for a debt problem?
In a recent year, 1.6 million families—fewer than 2 percent of us—voluntarily sought counseling for financial problems. The average debtor seeking help owes more than $20,000.

Ever contacted a company offering to clean up your credit record?
Only 6 percent have responded to offers to tame the debt monster.

Ever had the magnetic stripe on the back of your credit card fade?
More than half of us (54.2 percent) have had the frustration of discovering our magic money card is a dud, a worthless piece of plastic.

chapter 17

Love and Money

The pundits who claim love and marriage go together like a horse and carriage have forgotten the third leg of the stool. It's love, marriage, and money that make the world go round. Indeed, few other ingredients can strengthen or splinter friends and lovers as much as money.

Who in your pas de deux does the checkbook and bills?
Must be a girl thing. In households where money is pooled, three out of five women are solely responsible for balancing the checkbook and 56 percent pay the bills.

Who does the budget?
Like mowing the lawn and taking out the garbage, this one goes in the guys' column. Just over one-third of women—38 percent—say they're captain in this arena.

Would you lend your spouse for $1 million?
Two-thirds of us, holding tight to those holy vows, wouldn't lend our spouse for a night, even for a million bucks. One in ten would

accept this indecent proposal, while 16 percent admit they'd mull it over. Another 13 percent aren't talking.

Who makes the big bucks in your family?
Overwhelmingly, it's still the men who bring home the bacon—or at least more of it than the women. But one in four women in dual-earner couples now earns more than her hubby.

Think a woman earning more than her hubby spells trouble?
Some 53 percent of women and 34 percent of men feel that women bringing home more dough would lead to dissension.

Would you sign a prenup?
One in three of us think that all couples should sign a prenuptial agreement and that it's the best way to avoid fighting over money if they split. Sixty-eight percent of women and 63 percent of men won't sign one but just 36 percent overall say they'd flat-out refuse if their partner proposed it. This requires some finesse.

Would your partner sign a prenup if you had more assets?
Forty-four percent of women trust that their intended would do the right thing, but 25 percent think Romeo wouldn't.

Does the value of an engagement ring matter?
Seventy-eight percent of romantics say no.

How much did that wedding set you back?
If you married recently, chances are your wedding cost an average of $20,000 (including the catering and cocktails). Some 2.4 million weddings each year fuel a $45-billion-a-year industry. The average cost of a honeymoon: $3,657. Some 99 percent of newlyweds take one.

Do you know how much your spouse makes?

What we make is apparently the last taboo. Three out of ten husbands and wives are in the dark. Our collective shyness or secretiveness about what we take home extends to other family members. Just 26 percent of moms and 19 percent of dads know how much their kids earn, and 19 percent of children know what their parents make. We'd rather talk about a friend's marital problems than shaky finances (55 percent to 47 percent).

Do you share your PIN numbers with your mate?

Fourteen percent of us would not trust our nearest and dearest with our personal identification numbers.

If you borrow money from your mate, do you pay it back?

Just 30 percent diligently do.

When a friend asks to borrow money, do you lend it?

Friendship is a pretty powerful force. Some 59 percent of us will lend money (perhaps grudgingly), depending on the circumstances. Twenty-three percent fork it over and then write it off mentally as a gift. Ten percent lend it with the full expectation of getting it back—or harassing the borrower if they don't. Yet 8.5 percent of us won't even lend dough to our parents.

When you eat out with friends, how do you usually split the check?

Go ahead and order the lobster. Almost half of diners (47.6 percent) divvy the tab equally. For 21 percent, whoever is treating treats, while 27.2 percent chip in proportionally to what they ordered. Some 4.3 percent find this situation so ticklish they "stay out of it and give what I'm asked for."

Date time: Who should pay?

Despite the concept of equality, more than half of us—54 percent—say the guy should almost always underwrite the event. But 31 percent believe they should go Dutch, and 13 percent believe that if the lass earns more, she should fork over the dough. Others grumble that the thing to do is split it or take turns.

How about when she invites him to dinner?

Two-thirds of people say when the woman does the inviting, she pays.

With friends do you keep a running mental score of who pays for what?

Forget about mental: A few of us (3.5 percent) actually write it down. Forty-four percent figure it all washes out in the end, while 20 percent feel that friendship is more important than who pays more.

If a friend were leeching from you, would it ruin the relationship?

Friendship can take a lot of abuse, but not the financial kind. Half of us (49.2 percent) feel that someone leeching off us would put the kibosh on a relationship: We'd feel used. Another 25 percent figure that while it may not happen right away, ultimately the behavior would ruin things.

Sex or money: Which do you argue about more?

Money is the number-one cause of disagreements in marriages, sparking nearly twice as many rows as sex. One in seven of us feel money generates daily stress in our lives. Twenty-nine percent of couples say they frequently disagree whether to spend or save money, beating out what to watch on TV as fight fodder.

What's the row about: How much to spend or what to spend it on?

Most money fights are about what to spend it on. Twenty percent of couples can't agree on financial goals. Fourteen percent of family feuds occur when the husband believes his wife spends too much, while 11 percent are caused by wives blaming their husbands for overspending. Another 11 percent of disputes arise over how much money a family can afford to save.

> More than one-third of women consider having enough money more important than good sex to the success of a marriage.

Should married folks keep separate accounts in their own names?

More than two-thirds of us (69 percent) think it's perfectly all right for a husband or wife to have an account outside joint terrain, while 24 percent think it indicates lack of trust. Twenty-eight percent believe such behavior leads to relationship problems.

Do you and your partner keep separate accounts?

More than one-third of us (36 percent) have both a separate and joint account. Twenty-five percent have only a joint account. Twenty-two percent keep separate accounts. (The rest are single.)

Should the partner who makes the lion's share of the family dough be entitled to make the lion's share of decisions?

Political correctness wins out, with 70 percent insisting decisions should always be made jointly. Twenty-five percent believe money should talk.

Who wins in money spats?

Thirty-three percent of both husbands and wives say they usually do. One-third of both sexes contend that usually nobody wins: The disputes don't get resolved at all.

Do you consult with your spouse before buying something big?

For the most part, couples seek consensus on items that cost more than $134, on average. But 62 percent buy their own clothes without consulting their significant others. And just over half purchase their own jewelry alone.

Is it OK to marry for money?

According to a Prudential survey, only 12 percent of women and 16 percent of men think it is. At the same time, 33 percent of women and 26 percent of men think it's very unwise to marry someone who'd be a financial albatross.

chapter 18

Take This Job and...

Some people work to live; others live to work. Where are you along the continuum? For all the talk about people willing to make less money and throttle down to avoid burnout, it seems a lot of folks are just as eager to go for the gold. Some 42 percent would rather toil fourteen-hour days for maximum pay than scale back for less money. Slightly less than one in five would rather work eight-hour days for 30 percent less compensation. And 19 percent would opt for ten-hour days for 20 percent less than they're now making.

Which would you pick?

... Cash bonus or vacation time?
Fifty-nine percent of workers opt for more vacation time.

... Work from home sometimes or receive more pay?
Sixty-one percent of us would rather work in our PJs.

... More money or a company car?
Money wins hands down (63.6 percent) over wheels.

... More money or bring your pet to work?

Amazingly, 10.4 percent would rather Rover not get lonesome.

Are you satisfied with the pay?

Fifty-three percent of employees have no gripes about what they bring home and 2 percent feel they are paid more than they're worth. Interestingly, how people feel about what they earn has little to do with what's actually in the envelope: Low wage earners are as likely as big earners to say they are overpaid.

Are you earning what you expected when you began?

Forty-three percent of workers take home less than they imagined they would when they started out. On the other hand, 32 percent earn more money than they foresaw. Only 21 percent are just about on track. Women tend to anticipate they'll make less than men ($32,800 versus $55,600). But they're just as likely as the guys to feel they're paid what they're worth.

Does good pay make up for a lousy job?

Four out of ten workers have stayed in a situation that was bad because the money was good. Men are more likely than women to put up with a job for the money (43 percent versus 37 percent), as are folks younger than fifty.

Would you keep your job if your salary were cut 25 percent?

Thirty-one percent would take that job and shove it. Another 55 percent say they'd take the salary cut and swallow it.

Have you asked for a raise in the past year?

Just 20 percent of men and 24 percent of women workers have. It seems employers are more responsive to men. Research shows their request is granted 59 percent of the time, versus 45 percent for women.

Other than not being paid better, what ticks you off?

There are, of course, a whole bunch of little grievances that really irk us on the job. Thirty-five percent of workers are seriously mad about employers scrutinizing and disallowing expenses, while another one-third are miffed by their lack of workplace privacy. Twenty-six percent are driven to distraction by a dirty office, and 21 percent by noise and windows that don't open. Five percent are piqued that they can't see the sky from where they sit, while 6 percent are irked that the office is mandated smoke free. Thirteen percent are ticked off by stale M&Ms in the vending machine.

If money were not an issue, would you continue to work?

Twenty-five percent of us would stay the course, but considerably more—39 percent—would throttle down to work part-time. Twenty-one percent say they'd cash in their chips and retire.

Think it would be easy to find a new job if you lost this one?

Nearly three-fourths of us feel we'd be up the creek. Blue-collar workers are especially antsy.

If fired, how long could you maintain your standard of living?

Twenty-two percent of us feel we've got enough stashed away to last indefinitely. Another 16 percent could last a year without a change in lifestyle, and 21 percent, a few months. But 39 percent couldn't get by for a month without making changes.

Getting any? Stock options, that is?

It's still a relatively rarefied group, with 17 percent of large companies granting options to at least half of their staffs, up from only 6 percent in 1993. Two-thirds of companies with fewer than 100 workers awarded options to all their employees.

Expect a bonus this year?

Only 31 percent of us figure we'll be so lucky. Full-timers are most likely to get one: Thirty-nine percent expect a little extra at year-end, versus 13 percent of part-timers. And 44 percent of those earning more than $100,000 take a bonus for granted, compared to 19 percent of those making less than $25,000. One-third of college grads expect they'll have a little something extra to send back to their alma mater this year. When it comes to the sexes, it's men first: Thirty-five percent figure they are bonus-bound, compared to 26 percent of women.

How much?

One-fourth of women with visions of green dancing in their heads are seeing little guys: They expect to get less than $100 as a bonus. Only 7 percent of men anticipate such a puny thank-you. Twenty-six percent of men and 32 percent of women expect to be stuffing their wallets with between $100 and $500, while 10 percent will take home the grand prize of five grand or more. In fact, most bonuses (64 percent) will be less than 10 percent of a worker's salary.

Whatcha gonna do with it?

Forty percent expect to save at least some of it. Women are more likely than men to blow the entire windfall (71 percent versus 55 percent). Fifteen percent imagine they will put the money toward a vacation, and 3 percent will donate at least some to charity.

Do you spread the word?

After the payoff, most people tell their partners first (64 percent). Parents are the next most likely to hear the news (15 percent), followed by friends (14 percent) and siblings (10 percent). Fourteen percent keep mum about this good fortune.

When you switch jobs, what do you do with the 401(k) holdings?

Take the money and run seems to be the order of the day. Some 68 percent of job changers opt for cash payments, and only one-third reinvest those balances in IRAs or the 401(k) plans of their new employers. The smaller the balance, the larger the likelihood the participant will opt for the cash.

Do you keep a home office?

Thirty-one percent of us have one. We shell out, on average, $3,500 to set up shop at home.

What other benefits does your company offer?

Eighteen percent offer domestic-partner benefits. Eighty-two percent offer tuition reimbursement, while 57 percent provide vision-care coverage. Six percent offer credit union services.

Would you sacrifice a high salary for stock options?

Most of us want cash on the barrelhead.

How much would it take for you to take this job and shove it?

Two of every three workers say they would walk off their jobs if a competitor offered a salary increase of as little as 10 percent.

A company Christmas party, or a $100 gift certificate?

Some 78 percent declined the festivities for the cash.

chapter 19

Kid$

A ssume the child goes to public school, has nothing seriously *wrong physically or mentally that requires costly correction, and can actually make it to adulthood without having to fly planes or ride ponies. You're still talking about an outlay of* well over $200,000 for just the basics: food, clothes, orthodontia, summer camp. Are the little darlings worth it?

What's the key factor in choosing your kids' pediatrician?

Whether Dr. X accepts our insurance coverage is the most important factor in deciding whether we visit (58 percent), followed by how convenient it is for us to get there—followed by the doctor's experience, how accessible he or she is after-hours, and recommendations from friends or family members, in that order.

As a kid, did you get an allowance?

Parents are all over the map on doling out the dough to kids. Twenty-eight percent recall that they got an allowance in line with what other kids got, while 19.6 percent are still miffed, years later, that they got less than the going rate. Twenty-seven percent never got an allowance—their parents just gave them whatever they needed whenever they needed it—while 25.6 percent had to earn all their own pocket money.

Do you give your kids an allowance?
About half of all the twelve-to-eighteen-year-olds in this country—some 10 million—receive an allowance as well as regular handouts from their parents. Overall, teens in the Pacific and Mountain regions are likelier to get an allowance and parental cash infusions than Southerners.

How much do you give your kids as an allowance?
It pays to be a kid. The median amount of allowance these days is an astonishing $50 a week. Those in the Northeast corridor receive the most (a median $75 a week), while teens in the Southeast get the least. Generally, the richer the household, the higher the teen's allowance.

At what age did the allowance start?
For most, the largesse begins at six to eight years old but for 8.6 percent, the tap turns on before they're five years old, while 23.6 percent have to wait until nine. For 11.3 percent the magic age is twelve.

Was the allowance you got or gave your child tied to chores or grades?
Dr. Spock might be turning over in his grave about this, but 43.7 percent of us tie allowance to chores. Just 16.5 percent say they've read raising-kids guides that say this is a bad idea. The rest either never gave or received an allowance or tied it to chores to a very limited degree. Only 5.8 percent of parents admit they consider an A worth some legal tender.

Have you told your kids how much you make ... or did your parents tell you?
Not likely. The kids probably know more about your college

escapades than your current income. Just 9 percent of us have been absolutely straight with the kids here, while 28 percent give a "broad strokes" overview. Some 17 percent tell the kids no need to worry, and 6 percent don't answer the question—or lie.

When your kids ask for frivolous stuff, how likely are you to oblige?

If the kids are spoiled, you know whom to blame. Sixteen percent of parents—or should I say patsies—admit they try to buy their kids the things they want most of the time. The rest hold their ground, albeit shakily.

Do you make your kids either earn or save for something big?

Eighty-eight percent say they insist on it.

Have you helped your kids set up a bank account?

Seventy-two percent have.

How much do you pay for a baby-sitter?

Nationwide, baby-sitters earn an average of $4 an hour (about the same as pet sitters). It varies depending on the sitter's age and where you live. Urban sitters get a whole lot more.

Should kids be taught personal finance at school?

An overwhelming 95 percent of us say yes, it's an important lesson for kids to learn when they're young. But 3 percent say children will have plenty of opportunity to learn their financial ABCs later on. And 2 percent are indignant at the idea that little Johnny would be calling his broker at lunch.

Who paid your college tuition?

Call it daddy's last largesse, but one-third of students' parents funded it. Another one-third's parents chipped in. Fourteen percent relied on student loans and 6.6 percent on scholarships,

What does your teen have?

Some 40 percent of twelve-to-nineteen-year-olds have a credit card, 14 percent have access to a department store card, and 11 percent have access to a bank card.

Some 57 percent of eighteen- and nineteen-year-olds have their own checking accounts.

Fifteen percent of teens own stocks or bonds, and 7 to 11 percent, mutual funds. Just over 1 percent own CDs—the financial, not musical, kind.

Nearly one-third of teenagers hold part-time jobs.

while 12.6 percent financed college in other ingenious ways. Do you watch *The Sopranos*?

Ready to foot the college bills?
Fifty-eight percent of America's parents suspect that their savings won't be enough to cover the costs of college. Some 56 percent have no formal financial plan for funding their children's college education.

Do your kids help pay for their tuition?
Help? Thirty-five percent of our kids say they pay it all. One-fifth say they help by working, and 19 percent say scholarships have contributed. The rest leave it to Mom and Dad or the finance company.

chapter 20

Retiring but Not Shy

The median age for retirement today is around sixty-three. But two out of five of us fully expect to hang it up before we turn sixty-two. According to the American Academy of Actuaries, one-third expect to wrap up their primary careers by age sixty. With life spans stretching like mozzarella, will these elongated retirement years actually turn out to be golden?

Do you expect the golden years to be that ... or just plain gray?

Some 59 percent of us expect that our standard of living will be lower than it is now. But 21 percent anticipate it will actually rise.

Figured out how much you'll need to retire?

One-third of us haven't the foggiest notion how much we'll really need.

How much are you kicking in to make those pastures green?

What we're putting aside is very modest: The median annual contribution to retirement savings is only $3,000.

Think that's enough?

Well, think again. The average preretiree will have accumulated just $380,000 by age sixty-two, including home equity, savings, and the future value of pensions and Social Security. That's hardly enough to maintain the status quo. While 51 percent of us believe we're behind in our retirement saving—optimists till the end—only 25 percent feel they can't catch up.

Are you worried about outliving your retirement savings?

At the same time, 45 percent of workers worry that they'll last longer than their dough. (Only 31 percent of current retirees feel that way.)

Have you opted out on a retirement plan?

One in ten employees whose companies make automatic contributions for them opt out. Eighty-seven percent of those who can participate do so. But lots aren't entitled, because only half of Americans have a 401(k) plan.

Are you paying a fee to your company for handling your 401(k)?

More and more of us are, whether we know it or not. In 1999, 38 percent of companies with 401(k) plans charged participants record-keeping fees, up from 22 percent in 1991. But most participants don't know they're paying, because companies disclose administrative fee information only on request.

If you moved your 401(k) money, why'd you do it?

Sixty percent of plan participants have at one time or another moved their money. Twenty-eight percent went for the gold: better investment options, lower fees, or both. Thirteen percent wanted to simplify, to consolidate retirement money in one place. Nine percent had to move—their old plans wouldn't let them stay—while 1.5 percent felt they were pushed: The plan changed managers, and they didn't like the new options.

Got an IRA?

Just 23 percent of folks have one through their employers or privately. Of those who do, seven times more have traditional IRAs than Roth IRAs.

Twenty-six percent of folks believe they'll need at most $100,000 to maintain their current lifestyle once they've retired. Some 42 percent expect they'll need $100,000 to $500,000, and 24 percent figure $500,000 to $2 million. Nine percent anticipate they'll need more than $2 million to continue to lead the same kind of life.

Do you expect to have it?

Sixty-six percent expect to have what they need when they need it, but 29 percent aren't so bullish. Five percent either don't know or aren't telling. Forty-four percent of current retirees who had a retirement savings goal failed to reach it.

Are you counting on the pension plan?

Like one of your ten fingers. Seventy-four percent of workers are counting on their pension plans for some, if not all, of their retirement income. Fifty-five percent expect their employers will also provide health care coverage after they've retired.

When did you start stashing some away for those golden years?

Traditionally, the median age people began saving for retirement was thirty-four. But that age has been dropping. Sixty-four percent began as early as twenty-three.

Do you keep raising the bar for how much you'll need?

Two-thirds of us keep upping that magic number in our minds that we'll need to reach to retire.

Think Social Security will be there when you are?
Dream on. According to the Employee Benefits Research Institute, 96 percent of current workers won't be eligible for full Social Security benefits when they reach sixty-five, but only 16 percent realize this.

How much is in your 401(k) account?
The average account balance is near $40,000, according to a Federal Reserve survey. Just 10 percent have more than $100,000.

When you're ready to retire, what will you do with your dough?
Historically, 49 percent have rolled their money into IRAs; 24 percent have taken the cash.

In a recent survey of eighteen-to-thirty-four-year-olds, 46 percent believed in the existence of extraterrestrials, but only 28 percent believed Social Security would still be around when they're ready to cash in.

Expect to work after retirement?
Sixty-four percent of us plan to remain in harness in some manner.

Ever dip into retirement savings to satisfy a whim?
Fifteen percent of folks have tapped their retirement savings in the past three years to buy a new car. Twelve percent each have dipped in to treat themselves to a big luxury or fund a vacation.

chapter 21

Home: Castle or Money Pit?

They say a man's home is his castle. They also say it's a money pit. In either case it's probably not the one he or she grew up in—or, for that matter, started out married life in. According to U-Haul, the average American relocates eleven times over the course of a lifetime—buying and selling a fair number of houses along the way.

Own one?
A record 67.2 percent of families own a home—more than at any other time in history, according to the U.S. Department of Housing and Urban Development.

Ever spent more on anything?
It's the biggest single purchase 83.5 percent of us have ever made—or ever will.

What would you rather spend it on?
Not much. Ninety-one percent of us would rather own a home

than drive a better car, and two-thirds would defer their retirements for a decade to be a home owner.

OK, so is it a money pit?

We shell out nearly one-third (32 percent) of everything we spend on that roof over our heads—and the stuff it protects. Home owners spend on average $1.50 for every $1 a renter spends.

What the biggest threat to the value of your home?

Forty-three percent of home owners think it's fire. But exterminators say termites are the top threat to the value of homes—striking more than five times as many homes each year than do fires.

> The median price buyers paid for a home in a recent year was $134,300—meaning that half of all houses nationwide sold for more and half for less. The average monthly payment for all home buyers was $1,240.

How much did you look before buying?

The average shopper considers 14.5 houses before picking one to live in, according to Chicago Title and Trust Co. Both first-time and repeat buyers spent, on average, 4.8 months looking.

Who decided which house to buy?

When it comes to couples, 48 percent claim it's a joint decision. When one spouse was responsible, more often it was the woman.

Did you have it inspected before signing?

Most people do have a presale inspection, at an average cost of $250 to $400. HouseMaster, a home inspection company, says that 40 percent of resale homes have at least one major defect.

Got a mortgage?
Thirty-seven percent of people own their homes outright, free of that monkey on their backs.

Did you get a mortgage the first time you applied?
Sad to say it, but if you're black or Hispanic, the answer is far likelier to be no than if you're white. According to the Federal Financial Institutions Examination Council, whites got turned down 25.5 percent of the time, blacks 49 percent of the time. Native Americans were turned down 42.1 percent and Hispanics, 35 percent of the time.

Did you prepay your mortgage?
Seven percent of home owners did the ultimate prepay: They never even took out a mortgage, paying cash for their homes instead. Of those who did it the more conventional way, more than 70 percent have prepaid at least one mortgage payment.

Whose name is the lead on the mortgage application?
When it comes to researching the mortgage, 55 percent of the women get stuck with that job. But men's names are the "lead" on 74 percent of couples' mortgages, making them the primary borrowers on mortgage applications.

Applied for a mortgage online?
People shopping for mortgages regularly go online to compare rates and get information. But only 4 percent of recent home buyers applied for a mortgage online. And just 2 percent actually closed a loan on the Internet.

How much did you put down?
Recently, the average down payment was 19.5 percent of the sale price nationally.

How long did you save for the down payment?
First-time buyers saved on average 2.2 years for it.

Three percent of Americans have an in-ground swimming pool, game/billiard room, Jacuzzi bathtub, or fireplace. Five percent have cathedral ceilings or skylights, and 11 percent, a workshop or hobby/studio. Two percent have a gym or fitness room, and 1 percent a greenhouse, sauna/steam room, or wine cellar.

Ever refinanced your home?

It may be the money pit, but one-third of us have no intention of slithering in any deeper. Thirty-two percent of us have not refinanced our homes and don't plan to. Thirty-eight percent have done so once, and 14 percent have done it at least twice.

Do you own a second home?

Only 6 percent of us own second or vacation homes.

What's in the dream house?

More than anything else, we want a state-of-the-art kitchen. According to Roper Starch Worldwide, 29 percent of Americans yearn for a designer cooking space, while 27 percent hanker for a Jacuzzi, and 26 percent each, a fireplace, pool, and walk-in closets.

Any improvements planned?

Forty percent of homeowners expect to make some changes around the house soon. Based on what got the heave-ho in the past, kitchens are the likeliest choice for serious renovation (15.3 percent).

How much do you expect that will set you back?

In a recent year we spent, on average, $2,888 sprucing up our homes. Some 43 percent went toward interior decoration, 34 percent to landscaping, and 11 percent to expansion.

How many bids do you get before a big renovation project?

More than half of us get at least three bids before the walls come tumbling down, while two-fifths say they get two and then pick. Only 6.7 percent take the first bid presented to them.

What did you spend most on in the house?

Americans, it seems, are torn between comfort and a good time. Some 24 percent say they've spent more on their bedroom furniture than anything else, while an almost equal number—23 percent—have shelled out more on their entertainment centers than anything else. For 17 percent the costliest home furnishing was the sofa, and for 15 percent, the music system.

Ever paid for a professional designer or interior decorator?

Just 15.6 percent of us have. Of those who did, 22 percent would not make the same mistake twice.

Do you hang bills on your refrigerator door?

Along with other relics from the family museum, including photographs, children's artwork, and "to do" lists, bills are tacked to the fridge door by 10.3 percent of us.

When something goes wrong, who ya gonna call?

Not Ghostbusters to replace a broken window or cracked tile. Some 38 percent of home owners would try to make minor repairs themselves, while 31 percent would turn it over to their significant other. Twelve percent would call a repair person, while 18 percent would put it on a list of things to do that they admit they'll probably never get to. Two percent say they'd go into denial and acclimate to living without the broken item.

Did your home come with a warranty?

If you bought it recently, there's a one-in-four chance it did.

Do you have loss-of-use insurance on your home?
Huh? you say—until flood or fire or other catastrophe sends you packing to somewhere else you can hole up during renovations. Half of us don't know what loss-of-use insurance is, while 32 percent say they learned the hard way to request it. Nineteen percent knew about it but didn't want to pay the premium.

Have you tried to save the hefty broker commission by selling your house yourself?
In the trade it's called FSBO, pronounced "fizzbo" and meaning for sale by owner. Each year, 15 percent of the 5.6 million home owners who put houses on the market try to save the broker's commission by being their own broker. Bad idea, warns the National Association of Realtors (unsurprisingly). Many fizzbo sellers price their homes too low—and fail to sell at the peak profit.

Ever had your home appraised just to see what it was worth?
Sixty percent of us have gotten real estate brokers' juices salivating under false pretenses. Twenty-five percent consider that a frivolous waste of time. Sixteen percent couldn't do it if they wanted to: They don't own their own home.

What's the most monetarily stressful situation?
Forget taxes, babies, and weddings: The big fiscal flummox comes from buying a house. Thirty-three percent of us say that's the top financially stressful event.

chapter 22

You Paid *What* for Club Med?

Sun and surf, ski and sled, hike and bike—it doesn't matter what you do for fun. Chances are it costs money. Big time. But how you dole it out can make all the difference—or at least tell a lot about your personality.

Assuming you have time, would you take a one-stop flight on a carrier where you have miles or a nonstop flight on another airline?
Need proof that miles matter? Almost two-thirds of us (63.8 percent) would opt for the one-stop plus miles.

Would you sit in the middle coach seat of a cross-country flight or pay $100 more from your own pocket to fly business class?
Apparently not everyone knows how agonizingly long a cross-country flight can be. Some 54.8 percent of us would take the middle seat rather than spring for the upgrade.

Would you take a middle seat on a jammed four-hour flight and get frequent flier miles or a window or aisle seat on a less-crowded airline leaving at the same time? Comfort wins ... but not by much. Sixty percent of us would scurry to the other carrier.

Do you conscientiously set money aside for vacations? More than half of us (52.8 percent) don't have anything as specific as a vacation fund. Just 19.4 percent conscientiously earmark money for getaways.

How much do you think you spend on vacations? On average, we spend just $3,129 on entertainment and vacations in a year. The average summer vacation costs around $2,300, about 8 percent of the average American's annual income.

How much cash do you usually take on a trip? Two-thirds of international travelers head off with less than $100.

Do you still buy traveler's checks when you go on vacation? Twenty-two and one-half percent still do.

Do you try to figure out how much the trip will cost before you go? Just 8 percent of us set off on a vacation without any idea whatsoever of how much it will set us back.

Do you try to prepay most of a trip before going? It's why Club Med is so popular. More than one-third of us (36 percent) usually try to prepay most of a vacation. Another one-third (33.8 percent) rarely if ever do and are philosophically opposed to the lack of spontaneity that describes.

How do you typically pay for stuff on a trip? The card's the thing. Eighty percent of us slap down a credit or debit card to pay for the room, 75 percent to buy the airline seat, and 71 percent to rent a car. Forty-three percent of international travelers believe we're moving to a cashless society; 16 percent believe cash is already obsolete.

Ever cut a vacation short because you ran out of money?

That horror has happened to 3 percent of us. And more than 14 percent say they've economized in the waning days of a vacation.

Are you in a frequent flier program?

No wonder it's almost impossible to cash in those miles. Around 70 million of us now belong to frequent flier programs—up from 53 million five years ago. Collectively our banked miles are growing by 400 billion a year, so it won't get easier to get a free flight any time soon.

How many frequent flier programs do you belong to?

The typical active traveler belongs to seven. There are more than ninety of these programs worldwide.

The average frequent flier earns about 12,000 miles a year. Some 123,000 people have earned at least 1 million miles.

Do you usually buy car rental insurance?

Savvy travelers, we: Two-thirds decline those hefty charges, secure in the knowledge that we are covered by our credit card.

Do you usually buy flight insurance?

More than three-fourths of us (79 percent) never do, figuring why root against ourselves. About 4 percent claim that although they don't buy flight insurance as a rule, they have done so when they've had an unsettling intuition.

Do you order room service when you're paying?
On a special occasion like a honeymoon, 51 percent of us say to heck with the charge. But one-third of us (33.8 percent) consider room service a decadent waste. Meanwhile, 15 percent find it such a treat that they order it regardless of cost.

chapter 23

Wheels

The average per-pound price of a new car is around $6.86. But few (if any) of us buy cars by their weight. Many of us do, however, buy them for what they say about us. For many, a car is a badge of identity. For others, it's merely a way of getting from one place to another. Naturally, how we view a car influences how much we spend to buy and maintain it.

Which grade of gasoline do you usually buy?
We may love our cars, but when it comes to filling up the tank, we economize. Some 61.4 percent of us always fill up with regular.

Do you comparison shop when buying a car?
Sixty-four percent of us shop around before purchasing a new car. That's more than the number of people who comparison shop when buying an electronic item like a cell phone or DVD player.

Did you buy or lease your last car?
In 1990, just 10 percent of those who shopped for new cars opted to lease instead of buy. A decade later, 32 percent did.

How much did you spend?

The average new car owner shelled out a tad more than $21,000 for his wheels. Typically, buyers spend at least 30 percent of their net worth on a new car.

Deep down, do you really like to haggle for a car?

Despite nearly a decade of predictions that one-price, no-hassle/no-haggle selling would become standard operating procedure, it hasn't happened. The reason: Car buyers don't want it to. While 39 percent profess they prefer to shop at a dealership featuring one-price selling, few actually buy there. Almost nine out of ten admit that after getting a quote from a no-hassle/no-haggle store, they shop around for a better deal.

> Overall, we spend 30 percent more on buying and maintaining our cars or trucks than on feeding ourselves. We spend 39 percent more on gas and oil than we do on beverages for ourselves.

Think you'd pay the same for a car on a lot as on the Web?

Thirty-three percent think we'd get a better deal on the Internet but only 1 percent have actually bought a car online.

What's the most important factor in clinching a sale?

Forget the souped-up engine or racing stripes. When it comes to making a deal, reliability for the best possible price—and not necessarily the best-looking car—is a closer.

Before buying a used car, would you have a mechanic inspect it?

One-half of buyers fear that the car they're about to buy has something mechanically wrong with it, but only one-quarter bring it in for a professional inspection before the sale.

Do you have your car serviced according to the manufacturer's guidelines?
Expense be damned: More of us have our cars serviced at the dealer than anywhere else.

There's more than $450 billion in car loans outstanding in America.

If you wanted to sell a car, what approach would you take?
Even though it's not exactly the best deal in town, 44 percent of us would bring it to the dealer for a trade-in. Another 36.7 percent would run a newspaper or Web ad to try to sell it themselves.

If a car you'd planned to sell needed repair work, what would you do?
They don't use the expression "Caveat emptor" for nothing. More than half of us—53.3 percent—would simply put the car on the market "as is."

Will your next auto purchase most likely be a new or a used car?
Forget about "preowned." More than half of us say if we're going to drive, let those wheels be shiny and new.

chapter 24
Yakkety Yak

Despite what the song says, we do talk back. More people have phones than cars, and boy, do we ever use them. Competition has made the price of chat tumble, but many people aren't even aware of how much they pay.

Do you have more than one number at home?
Seventeen percent of homes in America have at least two.

Ever switched phone companies to get a cheaper rate?
Thirty-nine percent of us have.

Ever had your phone service suspended for nonpayment?
Some 8.5 percent of us have. An additional 1 percent explain that "It's a very complicated story."

Let discounted pricing determine when you phone long-distance?
Thirty percent do wait until the discounted hours to dial.

Do you save your toll calls to make at work?
Diogenes lives. Half of us (48.1 percent) don't sneak our toll calls onto our employer's bill because it's dishonest. But 7.7 percent say they do so all the time. Another 6.5 percent would like to do so but are deterred because their phone calls are logged.

Do you even know what you're paying for your home phone?
More than one-third of us—37 percent—don't even pay attention to what our long-distance service costs. We just write the check and move on.

Do you try to keep your long-distance calls short?
The largest percentage of calls (34 percent) last no more than one minute. Most of those presumably go to answering machines. The

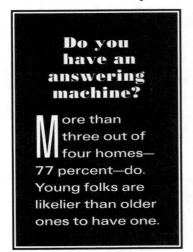

**Do you
have an
answering
machine?**

More than three out of four homes— 77 percent—do. Young folks are likelier than older ones to have one.

shortest calls tend to travel the fewest miles: For calls from one to ten miles, the average is 4.2 minutes ("Hello, Domino's?") The longest calls (an average of 11.8 minutes) spanned between 1,000 and 2,000 miles ("I just told you everything I put in my letter").

How much does your cell phone cost you?
The average price for cell service each month across four typical usage plans (30, 150, 300, and 600 minutes) was $40.64 in June 2000. Los Angeles is the most expensive city to call from the car.

Do you pay to be unlisted in the phone book?
Anonymity has its price! Only 25 percent of us are prepared to pay it.

Do you use e-mail instead of the phone to save moolah?
Almost half of us (45 percent) deny that's why we chat with our fingers, while 28 percent emphatically practice the technique to cut costs.

Ever call 1-900 numbers?
Ninety-two percent of people claim they've never dialed a 900 number.

chapter 25

The Soul of Generosity

The Bible tells us that jealously guarding what we have leaves us empty and craving for more ... but that the more we give to others, the richer we become. Our generosity is another litmus test of the soul. And it's not just how much we give, but how. Are you motivated by a sincere desire to help others—or by public recognition?

When the proverbial plate is passed, do you give?
Two out of three of us contribute to a charity in a typical year.

Do you give to beggars?
Begging is pretty profitable work if you can stand the ignominy. Thirteen percent of people claim to almost always give money to beggars when they come across them. Twelve percent donate if they're in the mood, and 7 percent decide based on the beggar's looks, clothes, smell, and gender.

Who are you giving to?
We give more money to the Salvation Army than to any other "offi-

cial" charity—and have done so for the past eight years. Runners-up, according to the Chronicle of Philanthropy, are the YMCA, Red Cross, the American Cancer Society, and the Fidelity Investments Charitable Gift Fund.

Do you want to be thanked and stroked by the charities you support?
Fifty-three percent of givers want an ongoing relationship with the recipients of their generosity.

> One-third of worshippers (36 percent) say they would keep their hands in their pockets when the collection plate came around.

Do you donate money anonymously?
Forget anonymity: Twenty-nine percent of us prefer to take the credit. Another 18.7 percent have gone undercover only when forced—when revealing themselves would have been embarrassing. Twenty-two percent don't donate at all.

What percentage of charity appeal mail do you read?
Charities waste a lot on paper and postage. Forty-six percent of us throw out almost all of it without a glance.

Do you tend to give where you've given before or to spread the wealth?
It's hard for a new charity to break in. Two thirds of us—65.4 percent—stick with where we've given before.

What's the best way to your wallet?
The envelope left on the table after a charity dinner is the most effective tug.

Ever contribute to political campaigns?
Two-thirds of us never ponied up any money for politicians.

Thirty percent of women and 26 percent of men turn out the lights and pretend not to be at home on Halloween, as do one-third of people sixty-five and over.

If recruited to fund-raise for a charity you support, would you?

Thirty-nine percent of us would grit our teeth and do it graciously. Twenty-nine percent would be too uncomfortable. Eighteen percent would embrace the mission and go all out, while 14 percent expect they'd procrastinate and make it up with their own check.

chapter 26

Tip-Top

ost people think "tip" has to do with advice, but the word actually originated in eighteenth-century England, where coffeehouse patrons were encouraged to put coins in a box labeled "To Insure Promptness." Researchers have found that people tip not just to say thanks or guarantee better service on a return visit but for all kinds of psychological power trips. Studies show that tips may have less to do with the size of the bill or the quality of service, and more to do with vagaries like the weather or the personality of the tipper.

Do you usually tip?
Ninety-four percent of folks who are served by waitstaff usually leave a little something to express their gratitude—or conformity.

Are you comfortable figuring out the tip?
Fewer than one-third of us profess to feel very competent here, especially when it comes to captains and wine stewards. Men, perhaps because of practice or natural feelings of superiority, claim to be slightly more adept at it than women (30 percent versus 25 percent).

Do you calculate tips on the pretax total?
Two-thirds of us make the calculation on the gross amount after tax.

In an expensive restaurant, do you tip differently?
Three out of four of us don't change the percentage we leave because of the venue, but one in four do—reducing the percentage somewhat. Similarly, in a cheap place, 61 percent tip the same percentage, whereas 39 percent increase it a bit.

About one-third of people usually leave 10 to 15 percent of the pre-tax total. Another one-third try to nail it at 15 percent. Twenty-one percent of us up the amount to 20 percent. Seven percent sheepishly admit that they leave closer to 10 percent.

Do you tip at take-out counters?
Eighty-three percent never leave a tip at a take-out counter, whereas 5 percent always do.

If the service isn't what it should be, do you tip less?
More than half of us—54 percent—scale back when the service doesn't meet our expectations. Twenty-three percent still tip the usual amount. Nine percent—punitive souls—leave nothing or pennies. Two percent say they speak with the manager.

How about if the waiter didn't offer to replace food you complained about?
Some 42 percent of people would trim the tip significantly if the waiter didn't do something about an unsatisfactory meal.

And if he or she didn't bring water when asked?
Twenty-seven percent of diners express their displeasure with water deprivation by shaving the tip.

What if the food wasn't good?
Twenty-one percent of restaurant patrons exact revenge on the server by leaving less.

If the server doesn't clear dishes promptly, do you trim the tip?
Just 8 percent of us think that sufficiently grievous to reduce the pourboire.

Do you tip the same even if you're not likely to be back?
Four out of five of us say the tip is a reward for past service, not a bribe for future favor. But 21 percent figure who's to know?

Do you tip more for tactility?
Perhaps you're not aware of it, but patrons do seem to tip

Would you tip more on a nice day?

You'd probably say that would make no difference. Wrong. When guests at an Atlantic City hotel with no outside views were told it was sunny when they received their breakfast tray, they tipped on average 29 percent of the bill. Those who heard it was rainy tipped 19 percent of the bill. Guests told it was cloudy tipped 24 percent, and those given a partly sunny forecast tipped 26 percent.

more if their waiter or waitress touches them on the arm or shoulder. An experiment in 1984 showed that food servers who touched their customers on the hand or shoulder when asking if the meal was all right, raised their tips on average 3 percent.

How about if the waiter introduces himself?

"Hi, I'm Candy" works, though you probably don't want to hear it. Waitstaff who introduce themselves by name report getting better tips, as do those who crouch at the table when taking an order instead of standing upright. Waitresses who put a smiley face on the bill increase their pay—but waiters who do usually wind up with less.

Do you tip more if the waiter writes "Thank you" on the bill?

Research says that on average, patrons increase their tips by two percentage points for such a personal message.

Do you tip more if you're paying by cash or by credit card?

Customers are unaware of any difference, but experts say that diners who pay with credit cards tend to tip more.

Do you tip more if the bill comes on a tray?

Just as the smell of fresh pine increases the sale price of a home, a little strategy like putting the bill on a tray jacks up the return. A decorated tray increases the tip most of all.

Does the number of people in your group affect how you tip?

People who eat by themselves are the best tippers, leaving an average tip of 19.7 percent, according to the NPD Group. The rate drops to 14.9 percent for four and 13.2 percent for five diners.

Do you tip taxi and limo drivers, hairstylists, parking valets, bartenders, luggage handlers, and maids?

Just half of us ever use a taxi or limo driver. Of those who do, only three out of four usually reward the driver with a tip. It's the same percentage for hairstylists, barbers, and parking valets. One out of four who uses a luggage handler at hotels or airports stiffs him. Twenty-eight percent of guests who stay in hotels never tip the maid.

If the staff pools their tips, do you leave less?
Two out of five of us trim their largesse.

Would you tip a hairstylist who owns the salon?
Two-thirds of customers don't care whether the stylist owns the joint or not: They'd tip.

Do you tip the attendant in a public restroom?
More than one-third of us (36.7 percent) rarely if ever tip the attendant. Twenty-three percent do so only when the attendant offers a towel, while 19 percent do so only if they can't escape it without embarrassment.

chapter 27

Taxed Out

A udits have been called autopsies without benefit of death, but even preparing the tax return itself is no picnic. Like death, it's been accepted as one of life's inevitabilities but certainly not one of its pleasures.

Do you file on time?
Almost everybody claims to. One-fifth (20 percent) get down to business right at the last minute, while only 1.6 percent will admit that they're usually one or two days late. Nine percent almost always get an extension.

How long do you keep your old tax returns?
It's no wonder we need basements. Some 43.2 percent of us keep returns forever, and another 37 percent hold on to them for seven years—after that they can't be audited. And 4.4 percent don't keep them at all: What tax returns? they wonder.

Do you know your tax bracket?
Apparently, 22 percent of us have no idea.

How long does it take you to do your taxes?
Longer than it used to. The IRS estimates that it will take a tax-payer 35.8 hours to fill out a Form 1040 and Schedules A through D, up from 30.6 hours five years ago.

Ever call the toll-free IRS "help" line?
In fiscal 2000, 79.6 million people did. A lot of them are wondering why they bothered. At least one-third of their calls went unanswered, the Treasury Department acknowledges. And 47 percent of the answers given were incorrect.

Are you taxed out?
Some 28 percent of Americans feel the tax burden is so onerous they've relocated.

How about stressed out?
Twenty-five percent of us say that preparing taxes is extremely stressful. Only 42 percent are confident that they fill out their tax forms properly, and 49 percent are less certain or even jittery. Ten percent confess they've not the foggiest idea what they're doing.

How do you feel about being audited?
Although the Internal Revenue Service audited fewer than 1 in 200 tax returns it received in 2000 (and won't disclose precisely how it targets them), the possibility of being in that one-half percent is traumatic. (Al Capone was supposedly a victim.) More people (30 percent) would rather take their chances in a car crash—assuming no one gets hurt—than be hit by an IRS audit (26 percent). And more (32 percent) would prefer to lose their wallet and credit cards and go through the ordeal of replacing them than go mano a mano with the tax man. Thirteen percent would even rather undergo root canal surgery than be subjected to IRS scrutiny.

If an audit happened, would you be prepared?
Only 32 percent of taxpayers have receipts to verify all deductions,

and only 40 percent say they can document most of them. Eight percent claim they can't account for any of their deductions.

Do you cheat on your taxes?
The government says it expects most people do, but only 4 percent of Americans admit they cheat on taxes. Fourteen percent say cheating is acceptable because the government's just going to waste the money anyway. Sixty-two percent insist it's never all right to shortchange the tax man.

How do you feel about paying taxes?
Although the IRS says 83 percent of Americans pay their taxes voluntarily, most aren't doing so happily. Sixty-nine percent believe that the rich get away with murder on their taxes, and 71 percent feel the same about corporations.

How do you feel about the whole tax system?
Eighty percent would like to see the system revised so everyone pays the same percentage in taxes, as they do in other countries. Just 20 percent want the IRS to keep its current policies.

What's the most irritating thing about doing your taxes?
Thirty-eight percent say it's watching how the government spends—or wastes—our tax dollars. Another 36 percent are most provoked by having to collect the necessary documents. For 21 percent the biggest problem is comprehending the IRS's forms.

Ever considered working as a tax collector?
Not likely. Only 11 percent would consider that versus 73 percent who would work in advertising (another vilified industry). But it beat out the 9 percent who'd contemplate being a garbage collector and the 7 percent who'd envision themselves as a proctologist.

Are you working for the tax collector?
Nationwide, the average person spends two hours and forty-six

minutes of an average eight-hour workday earning money that goes to pay federal, state, and local taxes. Put another way, Americans work an average of 124 days to earn the money to pay federal, state, and local taxes. It takes us, on average, until May 3 to earn the money to pay taxes, before we can start earning money for ourselves.

Do you usually get a refund?
Sixty-nine percent of us do. Recently the IRS said its average refund was $1,963.

Ever offered to settle this outside (that is, negotiate the amount you'll pay)?
In a recent year, the IRS accepted 26,668 offers of compromise out of the 99,078 filed, and it accepted about $287 million to settle debts totaling about $2.17 billion. The service does this when it has doubts about the taxpayer's liability or the collectability of the amount assessed.

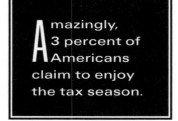
Amazingly, 3 percent of Americans claim to enjoy the tax season.

Do you pay a marriage penalty?
If you're married and file jointly you may be one of 25 million couples who now pay more in taxes than they would if they were single—$1,100 on average each year.

How much would it take to get you to file online?
While only 20 percent plan to file online this year, 43 percent would if offered a $10 tax credit for online filing.

Ever file a return and not sign it?
The IRS expects at least 8 million taxpayers to file with a missing signature or missing or incorrect Social Security number. In 1998, 270,000 people got a child's Social Security number wrong. Believe it or not, 160,000 flubbed their own Social Security numbers.

Do you intentionally overwithhold to get a refund?
More than half of Americans do (even though this is like giving Uncle Sam an interest-free loan).

Would you give up all government services in order to not pay income taxes again?
Seventy-three percent of us would not.

Do you look for loopholes in your taxes?
Twenty-eight percent of us are passionate about the search, while 43 percent embrace the loopholes if their accountant or someone else points them out. Another 28.9 percent profess disinterest.

chapter 28

Death Be Not Proud

Y ou can't take it with you. But that doesn't mean you have to spend it all before you go. And while you may not exactly be knocking at death's door, you know it's coming. So ... how financially prepared are you for the occasion of your own demise?

Where would you rather splurge: on a car or on a casket?
Drive, he said. Three out of five of us (61.7 percent) would go for the wheels over the box.

If you have a will, did you draw it up yourself?
Two-thirds of us paid a lawyer or other professional to draw it up. Twenty-one percent did it themselves, most often with the help of a do-it-yourself manual.

Who'll get the money?
More than three-fourths of us who are married list our spouse as the principal beneficiary. Almost as many include a "contingent

beneficiary," so if both die in an accident, the money will go directly to the kids or other designee.

Have you indicated who gets Rover?
One out of every four of us with pets has designated who gets Fluffy when we're no longer here to wield the pooper-scooper.

Are frequent flier miles figured in your will?
Ninety percent of frequent fliers don't refer to their miles in their wills. But estate (and divorce) lawyers value them at 2¢ each—the same amount on average that airlines charge when they sell miles to their corporate partners. Only about 10 percent of miles bequeathed to family, friends, or charities are ever claimed.

If you have children, should they inherit equally, no matter what?
Sixty-four percent of us say yes. But 25 percent believe it should be based on the individual child's needs. Ten percent feel it should be parceled out based on their feelings for their children. (So get on the phone and make nice.)

How much is your estate worth?
Despite all the talk about the burgeoning number of millionaires in this country, 93 percent of us have estates that add up to less than $1 million. One-fourth of will makers doubt they'll have anything to leave.

Do you have a will?

Despite the saying that where there's a will there's a way, more than 40 percent of people thirty-five and older don't have one. Amazingly, 40 percent of those who haven't made a will don't expect to do so before the Grim Reaper reaps them.

Do you expect to inherit money?

You should be so lucky, but two out of three of us really do expect that windfall at some point. The estimated median value of the inheritance: $135,000 from real estate, cash, stocks, or bonds.

Ever fought with your siblings over an inheritance?

One in three families squabble, sometimes ferociously, over what's left. Oddly, it's not money (which can be neatly divided) that causes all the bickering as much as household possessions.

Have you made—or do you expect to make—"preneed" funeral arrangements?

Not on your life, say two out of five of us (39.1 percent).

Burial or cremation?

The national average cost for a funeral, burial, and monument now runs around $7,520, depending, of course, on how memorialized you choose to be. At the same time, a typical cremation costs $1,000 to $1,400, including an urn and the process of returning the remains to the family or scattering them at sea.

Would you choose cremation because it's cheaper?

Almost half of us (47.4 percent) profess interest in cremation, but not because of the cost. Only one-fifth (20.8 percent) would opt for the ovens for purely monetary reasons. One-third (32.1 percent) want to be buried no matter what it costs.

Would you buy a worm-resistant coffin that's $1,000 pricier over one that lets the critters in?

Just over half of us have grown up believing the ashes to ashes, dust to dust bit from the burial rite of the Book of Common Prayer. Fifty-three percent wouldn't spend the money. Eighteen percent refuse to think about it.

Embalming's not required by law. Would you chintz here?

No one's looking, but only 18 percent of us would skip the transfusion for aesthetic or religious reasons. According to the National Funeral Directors, embalming will set you back anywhere from $369 to $625.

Going for a casket and vault?

Now you're talking real money. A casket usually goes for $395 to $10,000, while a vault fetches anywhere from $325 to $8,000. Vaults, or "outer burial containers," are often required by cemeteries to keep graves from caving in; that's their only use. No matter what the vault is made of, what's inside will still decompose.

What do you imagine you'll pay for a funeral service?

Expect to shell out anywhere from $225 to $650.

And a hearse?

More than you would spend for a limo ($75 to $260): A hearse usually goes for $135 to $345.

Any idea what "preparatory services" cost?

Figure on spending $50 to $185 to have the body bathed and another $50 to $185 to have it stored. Applying cosmetics for viewing will set you back another $50 to $185.

chapter 29

What, Me Worry?

Talk all you want about America's uneasiness with crime, it's money woes that are keeping folks awake at night. Five times as many of us worry more about our financial security than our physical safety. Are money worries keeping you up?

Is money an obsession or a passing blip?
One in five worrywarts confess that they often fret about money. Fifty-five percent think about it only when they're managing it, and 23 percent let their minds drift to it occasionally. Just 2 percent claim to have nothing to fear.

What do you worry about?
* Twenty-six percent of us get chills thinking about an IRS audit. Fourteen percent are frightened by the prospect of doing their own taxes.

* Thirty-six percent of us worry we won't be able to pay medical bills.

✳ Eleven percent of us dread having a credit card declined in public.

✳ Thirty-five percent of us worry that Social Security won't be solvent when we're ready to collect.

✳ Twenty-five percent worry about becoming the proverbial bag lady.

✳ Four percent worry that people won't like them because of how much or how little money they have.

✳ For 26 percent of us, the chronic inability to save money and pull ourselves out of debt is our single biggest financial worry.

✳ For 15 percent of Americans, getting the pink slip is the biggest financial fear.

✳ Thirty-nine percent worry they won't have enough to retire.

✳ Thirty-six percent worry about losing financial independence.

✳ Some 22 percent of us worry about having little or no inheritance to pass on to our children.

Twenty-three percent of people living down South named getting fired as their chief worry, compared to just 9 percent of Midwesterners.

✳ Thirty-one percent worry about being sandwiched between caring for elderly parents and taking care of our own kids.

✳ One in five actively worries about the turbulence of the stock market.

How do you cope with your money fears?

Slightly more than half of us (56 percent) retreat to the safety of bonds, treasuries, and caches under the mattress—or to the bottle, or friends, or whatever makes us feel better, reports Women.com. One-third read books and magazines to quell their fear. Six percent let their partner handle the finances. Two percent admit they're seeing a therapist.

> Almost two out of three people (64 percent) have modified their financial behavior in response to their fears.

About the Author

LEE WHITE

Bernice Kanner is the author of *The 100 Best TV Commercials...And Why They Worked, Lies My Parents Told Me,* and the original *Are You Normal?* She has appeared on *The Oprah Show,* NBC's *Dateline, The Today Show* with Bryant Gumbel, CNN, ABC *World News* with Peter Jennings, and dozens of other shows.

For thirteen years, Bernice Kanner served up an intimate look at the marketing world with her award-winning weekly column, "On Madison Avenue," for *New York Magazine. Forbes Media Guide* praised her "tireless legwork" and stylistic "aplomb," and noted "a Kanner column seldom fails to pique a reader's interest." At *New York Magazine,* senior editor Kanner was also a noted feature writer whose first-person adventures as a cab driver, traffic cop, Tiffany's temp, Wendy's counterman, census taker, Guerlain "nose," and Ritz Carlton concierge, among others, were some of the magazine's most celebrated pieces.

She has been a columnist and radio and TV commentator for Bloomberg and has contributed frequently to *The New York Times, The Sunday Times of London, Parade, Ladies' Home Journal, Working Woman,* and *American Demographics.* Before her stint at *New York Magazine,* Kanner wrote a daily column in the *New York Daily News,* was senior editor at *Advertising Age,* and worked at the J. Walter Thompson ad agency.

Get in *toon*
with your money

"I married you for your money, Leonard. Where is it?"

110 cartoons from the artists of *The New Yorker* on the influence, power, and occasional insanity of money in all of our lives

With a hilarious introduction by Christopher Buckley

Bloomberg PRESS

Available where books are sold or at www.bloomberg.com/books